RAISING

HOPE

Embrace a new perspective when faced with

an unexpected challenge

A true story of love, loss, and the power of choice

By

Laurice Duffy

Cover illustrated by

Terry Sabia

Praise for *Raising Hope*

"Our mother, Laurice Duffy is the most loving, wise, and strongest woman we know as she turned the death of our father/her husband into a positive by helping other women become the strongest, happiest version of themselves. She has taught us how to become great men without any help which is the biggest gift anyone has given us. We always knew our mother was tough, but to be able to deal with our dad/her husband passing away, and putting four kids through college while also taking care of her elderly father and still having time to have such an impact on her clients and others, is truly remarkable. We could not have asked for a better role model and leader."

Kelly, Tyler, Quinn
& Aidan Duffy

"A heart-opening book that is both inspiring and insightful. Laurice teaches us how we can approach life differently, no matter what circumstances we experience. I highly recommend it."

Patricia Keating, CEO
The Entrepreneur Unleashed

"*Raising Hope* is the perfect title for this inspirational book by my friend and neighbor, Laurice Duffy. After losing her beloved husband Kevin to ALS, Laurice found herself heartbroken, devastated, and overwhelmed. But she looked at her 4 beautiful sons and realized she needed to rise up and live life to the fullest. To choose happiness and to raise hope amid all the tragedy and loss... for herself, the boys, and in honor of Kevin.

"This is her remarkable, gut-wrenching, uplifting story, her journey from despair and loss to healing and hope. You will cry, laugh, and learn life lessons to take to heart in your own life challenges. As a widow, mom, and life coach, Laurice offers sage advice and helpful tips for women at all stages of life. A must-read to be the best you can be!"

Michele Treacy
Media & PR Strategist
Published Author

"A few things, words, and emotions touch your heart directly. You absorb them within yourself in such a way that they become an indispensable part of your identity. *Raising Hope* has done exactly the same thing to me. I came across this book when I had dived deep into the pits of darkness and depression. Many situations which Laurice explained throughout the book seemed so relatable that I could feel them happening around me. Then there came that point in the book when Kevin, the author's husband, started developing the symptoms of a cruel disease. My heart felt a pang of pain. I wanted to put down the book because I had no courage to read further. But the title of this book urged me to keep reading. I was stunned by Laurice's demonstration of bravery and resilience in this traumatic situation. What can be more agonizing than knowing that you are going to lose the most beloved person of your life at any moment? But the way Laurice embraced her destiny and moved on with life is something beyond words. Honestly, I was so overwhelmed that I couldn't help my eyes getting blurred with tears. However, despite having a myriad of emotions, the book is so reassuring that it feels like a breath of fresh air. The author definitely should take a bow for being such an inspirational writer and being a role model for so many. It won't be an overstatement if I say that *Raising Hope* has raised hope in my life without any doubt!"

Michelle Mourton
Senior Editor
Amazon Publishing Hub

"Laurice teaches us that hope is the best path forward following a life-changing event as devastating as the death of her husband and father of 4 teenage sons was from ALS. Rather than succumb to chronic despair and self-pity, she rises up and defines her mission to help others. This book challenges us to put our own setbacks in perspective and seek the light of hope. I encourage you to read and share this important book and keep the momentum of hope growing."

Anthony Coniglio, PharmD
Founder and CEO
OPUS Pharma Consulting, LLC

"Uplifted, inspired, hopeful! Just a few words to describe how you will feel reading this amazing journey of a family who went through the highs and lows life threw at them. You will laugh, cry and feel an amazing sense of hope. Laurice has captured perfectly how to breathe life into loss. The realness and the raw emotions she shares during this journey will deeply touch you and leave you with a feeling that no matter what loss you may experience in life you can find a hopeful light to guide you."

Mom of a child given a cancer diagnosis

"Laurice has gracefully found her way through some of life's heaviest circumstances, and now shares her wisdom and experience with others who are ready to rise above and start on their own path to a happy and fulfilling life. She's a powerful, compassionate and caring coach you can trust."

Ivana Siska Geier
Success Strategist &
Women's Business Coach

"My world turned upside down when I became a widow at 58. Working with Laurice has been an amazing life changing journey when I needed it the most!

She has helped me find strength I didn't know I had and the self-confidence to take on whatever the future holds with grace and honesty."

Gail Iriks
Widow

"Laurice Duffy lives her life on purpose, Driven and strong in face of tragic experiences with a touch of grace and understanding pulling everyone in her orbit closer. Through her word and action, Laurice has chosen to shine the light on the beauty of life. Laurice Duffy has never allowed life's circumstances to define her but chose to define her life by using her circumstance."

Kevin Donaldson
Host of *The Suffering Podcast*
www.Thesufferingpodcast.com
Co-Author of *Man You Are Crazy*
www.ManYouAreCrazy.com

"Laurice Duffy brings so much love, compassion and enthusiasm to her work. As one of her mentors in business, it was incredibly clear from the start, she truly cares for people and their journey. She's serious when she says she wants you to rise and believes in you even if you don't believe in yourself yet. When you learn her unimaginable story, you realize Laurice is a strong and powerful force, mom and inspired coach - meant to help others with her huge heart."

Elizabeth Walker
On-Camera and
Media Specialist

"Laurice takes readers on her heart-breaking journey through love, loss, and grief, in all of its complexity. She reflects on the struggles that many face, being a caregiver to her ill husband and raising her young children. This is a powerful example of what it means to find the strength to face each day and triumph over tragedy. Laurice shows us that despite all of life's difficulties, there is one thing we can always turn to -hope."

Jen Zwinck,
Host of *Widow 180: The Podcast*
Co-founder of *The Widow Squad Community*

"Laurice's raw words and experiences in HOPE have shown the readers that under any circumstance, we have the ability to choose who we want to be. She has shown us that it's not the obstacles in which our future is created, but the person we decide to be in each situation. Thank you Laurice for sharing your beautiful story of hope, love and inspiration."

Shari Rosenberg
Group Director of Private
Wealth Management Team

Raising Hope

Raising four boys with hope

in their hearts after losing

their dad, coach and

biggest fan

Raising hope for you, the reader!

No matter what challenges you face

Dedication

I dedicate this book to my courageous husband, Kevin Duffy. Your passing has taught me to live mindfully, show up fearlessly, and follow my dreams unapologetically.

Thank you for loving us so beautifully!

Contents

Foreword

There is no greater threat to hope than despair. If you are holding this book in your hands, perhaps you know this, not just intellectually, but in your bones. Perhaps you are intimately familiar with the suffocating, disorienting, all-consuming grief that tragedy can bring. If that is you, keep reading. This is a story you need to hear. The journey detailed in these pages describes the personal metamorphosis of someone who could have drowned in grief but who chose a different path. This is the story of a woman who found her meaning, her power, and her purpose in unthinkable circumstances. That woman, the book's author, is my father's youngest sister, my aunt Laurice. Laurice is one of those people with a natural ability not just to find but to crack open the joy of each moment. Navigating life with an aunt like Laurice is like learning to identify the calls of birds that frequent your backyard. It's easy for their sounds to fade into the background, but once you know what to listen for, the beauty that has surrounded you all this time is fully revealed. Laurice has an innate ear for the happiness and humor that are readily available if only we take the time to listen. As Laurice's second eldest niece, I have had the great fortune of being present for so many important milestones in my aunt's life. After I was born and she was just 24 years young, Laurice was my full-time caretaker when my parents returned to work. On days when I wish I could tell my younger self about what this relationship was going to mean to me, my message is something like this:

Dear Little Me,

I know it seems unthinkable right now, but in just one year, you are going to learn to walk. You are going to walk so well, in fact, that you'll be trusted to throw flower petals down the aisle at St. Anthony of Padua Catholic Church as Laurice marries the love of her life. Then, 8 years from now, you are going to visit your aunt at St. Joseph's University Medical Center after she gives birth to triplets. * *In the years to come, you will spend many weekends at your aunt's house helping care for these three babies and a fourth that will arrive a few years later. And, even though you'll be a preteen and can barely remember to change the family cat's litter box, let alone a diaper, and even though she is so exhausted, Laurice will be so glad to see you each time you arrive. She will make you feel so special and important. She'll ask you to bring your friends. She'll find time and energy to stock the freezer with homemade ice cream sandwiches. Twenty-nine years from now, you'll sit together on her couch in that same house, writing your grandmother's eulogy, eating more ice cream. And, while you won't be aware of it until much later in your life, she will be the one to show you how to respond to adversity with grace.*

It was both a tragedy and a privilege to bear witness to the story that Laurice describes in these pages. When my uncle was in the throes of his illness, I watched my aunt turn

---

* Unfortunately, you will faint during this hospital trip due to your crippling fear of needles. This is something to be addressed before you have children of your own

into a crumpled shell of herself, utterly defeated and hopeless. Indeed, as Laurice will describe in her own words, the tragedy of losing her husband to a disease as cruel and unsparing as ALS was not one that she initially met with hope. Hope was eclipsed by fear and anger at the injustice of these circumstances. It wasn't fair that four teenage boys, who only recently learned about ALS because of the then-popular Ice Bucket Challenge on social media, would soon learn that their father would succumb to this same disease. It wasn't fair that this same father, who, even after a hard day of work, always made time to play baseball with his boys, would die of a disease named after the famous first baseman Henry Louis Gehrig. It wasn't fair that a fatal disease, for which there is still no cure, counted this family among the many lives ALS upends.

During my uncle's initial diagnosis, I was in the early years of my graduate program, studying to receive my Ph.D. in clinical psychology. Although I would not confer with my aunt for many years later, I, too, was learning about hope and resilience, not from personal experience but from an academic one. I have amassed well over a thousand hours treating clients directly and at least another thousand studying them. In particular, my colleagues and I are interested in learning about how to predict who tends to lean into hopelessness as a result of their circumstances and who, instead, is resilient. I have learned what my aunt has intuitively known: hope is powerful.

Consider a study from 2016 where a group of researchers at the University of Michigan examined a large cohort of college students who had experienced traumatic events, such as physical assaults or natural disasters. Students who had experienced trauma and who tended to have low hope were the most likely to show symptoms of depression and anxiety, whereas students who experienced the same trauma but had more hope, were far less likely to develop such symptoms. The researchers found, in sum, that hope is indeed a thing to be raised.

The story you are about to read is remarkable on its own, and even more so because it is entirely true. It is the story of Laurice's journey to find and raise hope many times over in herself, her family, and now, in you. As you navigate these precious pages, Laurice's words make one thing abundantly clear: There is no greater threat to despair than hope.

Kathryn Coniglio, Ph.D.
Clinical Psychologist

About the Author

My inspiration for my career is deeply personal. From a young age, others have turned to me for counsel and advice. I later bolstered my innate listening and empathy skills with a BA in Psychology and a certification from the Institute for Professional Excellence in Coaching, which furthered my passion for empowering others to live and create their unique destiny. Although I've always found helping others meaningful, I couldn't have anticipated that my own life journey would shake up all of my assumptions and test my  resolve. My husband's battle with ALS and eventual passing was a turning point in my life. His illness shined a light on the limiting beliefs and behaviors I held close for so long, namely fear and grasping at control.

Letting go of these defense mechanisms was what ultimately unlocked my strength to move from darkness and despair into a place of peace and fulfillment. Experiencing this transformation in myself set me on a path to help others overcome adversity, tune into their power, and have a life of peace. I can relate to the many women who seek my services when they are feeling lost, living a life that looks good on paper but doesn't bring them joy. I, too, once lost myself in my role as a wife and mother, meeting the needs of others but letting my own slip by the wayside. I felt a strong pull towards a bigger life purpose, but society teaches women, especially mothers, not to ask for too much or dream too big. Having walked the same path as so many of my clients, I can offer empathy and compassion, as well as the wisdom and skills to guide them toward claiming a life that's more, no matter what circumstance they may be facing. I am motivated by leading women towards *a-ha moments* - those moments where your lens expands and you are able to let in new ideas, perspectives, and possibilities.

Those moments where a deeper, more purposeful life becomes possible. Witnessing these transformative moments in women and seeing them get unstuck is what tells me I have found my purpose in life. I experience deep meaning from working with women. I know that empowered women go on to inspire others and dream of a world where girls learn how to harness their power and create their own happiness from a young age. While my personal life is characterized by male energy, my career is where I tap into my uniquely feminine gifts. It's where I feel called to guide other women on a journey toward unlocking a peaceful life that is aligned with their true spirit. Where I feel connected to a sisterhood of women holding each other up and breaking down barriers.

Website:	www.amindfuljourneyld.com
Instagram:	www.instagram.com/amindfuljourney.ld/
Facebook:	www.facebook.com/amindfuljourneyld
Email:	amindfuljourney.ld@gmail.com

Introduction

It had only been two short months since Kevin's passing when a childhood friend approached me at her father's memorial and said, "you should write a book." Such a beautiful compliment! I loved the idea and her confidence in my ability, but I wasn't quite convinced I was up for the challenge. I had occasionally played around with the idea but actually doing it felt quite overwhelming. The topic came up more than a few times over the years, and I would think, "maybe one day." And then it came up again, and again and again. I wondered if I should be taking this consistent prompting more seriously. I strongly believe that the universe gives us a gentle nudge, a firm tap, and then a smack across the head! At this point, I had definitely received the nudge and the tap. However, on the 4th anniversary of Kevin's passing, I posted a blog in a large Facebook community. It was then that I received the smack in the head! So much kindness was shared with me in the comments of this blog about my beautiful ability to write. Some shared that they thought I was an author. Others wrote that it was the most thought-provoking and powerful post that they had ever read. And this was the moment when the thought, "How could I accomplish writing a whole book?" suddenly shifted to "How could I not?"

One important detail that needed clarity was the purpose of writing this book. What did I want to give to the reader? I knew immediately. Hope. The purpose of this book was to give the reader **Strength** and **Hope**. To be the reminder that it's not the tragic events we endure but instead the choices that we make following those events that shape our future. It's there where true power lives.

It was only weeks later that I sat down with a pen and notepaper. I outlined the topics for the book and typed into my phone calendar a deadline for each chapter. The first draft of my book was to be completed and sent to my editor the Tuesday following Labor Day. I sent it two days early. I've never experienced such ease as I did while writing this book. It was as if my fingers were dancing on the keyboards, pouring out a story that had already been written in my heart. I knew I was meant to write this book.

When we are born, each of us is given a chance to get in the game. With every new day, we get to choose how we're going to play that game. Do we ride the bench? Sit on the sidelines? Or do we sprint in and help the team?

My late husband Kevin showed up ready to play, ready to do his part. He didn't need to be the hero. He was happy to give his support however he could. Being on a team was special to Kevin – it meant being a part of something greater than himself.

Kevin gave 110% to every team he was on, every single day. As a senior in high school, Kevin was 5'8," 120 pounds, and an all-conference, all-county, all-state football player. His heart and love of the game were so much bigger than his physical size. Being a team player was the way he chose to live his life both on and off the field.

Growing up, Kevin's team was his mother, Patricia, his father, Jack, and two sisters, Kathleen and Jacqueline. They were a tight-knit team with a love of laughter and an unshakeable bond. Kevin's mom Patricia was a strong woman and a driven worker who instilled in Kevin a solid work ethic. Sadly, she passed away when Kevin was 23. Kevin had a close relationship with his father, Jack, which was made even stronger after his mother's early death. Jack never missed one of Kevin's sporting events. He was very proud of Kevin's character and accomplishments. Kevin also was blessed with two amazing sisters, Kathleen and Jacqueline, who would do anything for their baby brother.

After Kevin was diagnosed with amyotrophic lateral sclerosis (ALS), they were extremely supportive, involved, and committed to doing whatever was needed to get him better, including seeking out specialists and novel treatments and helping with their nephews' activities. Through all of the difficult times with Kevin's diagnoses and treatments, they stood by our side. They truly loved Kevin, and he knew it. We are blessed that they will continue to play an important role in our lives in the days, months, and years ahead.

When I met Kevin, I was immediately taken by his wide smile, joyful eyes, sense of humor, and infectious energy. He was a whistler, a singer, and a good morning guy, and the way he lit up a room - I knew I had found a very good man. And I knew if I became part of his team, he would be my partner, always show up, and would never let me down. And I was so right. Kevin often reminded the boys of how much he loved their mother, and every day I loved him with all my heart and soul.

As a father, Kevin didn't know the meaning of quitting. After a long day at work, hungry and tired, he would put food and rest aside for the chance to play basketball, have a catch, or throw a football with his boys. He loved each of them, Kelly, Tyler, Quinn, and Aidan, with an abundant, unending, joyful love and was grateful for and present in every moment he had with them.

He knew that spending time with them - whether it was family dinners, vacations, playing ball, coaching their teams, or just watching from the sidelines – amounted to more than just that one experience. He knew that each and every one of these moments was an opportunity to teach them. To model how to be a good man, respectful, and mentally tough. To model how to be a good father and husband. To model how to get in the game and to give your team 110% every single day.

He coached many boys on many different teams. I'm sure he coached many of you who are here today to celebrate his life. He encouraged, supported, and cheered for you. At times he helped you achieve your highest potential. And when you were down, frustrated, and ready to quit, he was there to remind you that your team needs you to stay in the game and give it all you've got.

Kevin also had strong beliefs and passions. In a land of NY Yankee and Met fans, Kevin was a diehard Boston Red Sox fan! That's how he lived, regardless of circumstances, challenges, or fears. He sprinted onto the field of life every day and played his heart out for his team – whether it be players, coworkers, or, most importantly, family and friends.

Today, I can choose to focus on what we've lost. But instead, I am choosing to be grateful to have had 28 years with my best friend, our biggest cheerleader, and the most amazing father to our four boys.

As he watches us now and sees that we're struggling and sad, I am certain he would remind us that the Duffy team needs the love and support of everyone who is here today. You are an important part of our team now. One day, our family will all be together again, but for now, the game must go on. We must show up for each other. We must support each other and sprint onto the field at every chance we get.

This was the eulogy that I read at my husband's funeral. Some called it courage. I called it love.

ONE

BEGINNING

I remember it like it was yesterday. I married the love of my life, and five years later, we were moving, along with our beautiful yellow lab Boomer, from our starter home to a new, larger home in the town where I grew up. We sold our house on our own to the very first couple that came to see it. I recall feeling so excited as I was packing up boxes, dreaming about the big family we would have in our new home. There was so much to look forward to. Our future looked so bright.

The phone rang in the midst of my elation. It was my husband's boss. He sounded very somber. "There has been an accident on the job, Laurice. A large pipe hit Kevin on the head. He's at the hospital." My brain stopped for a moment. I didn't know what to do. It's scary how life can change so drastically in an instant. I was so frightened but quickly called my parents. I was too shaken to drive. They came immediately, and we went straight to the hospital.

As I stepped into the emergency room, I was instantly met with the reality of my husband's serious head injury. The doctor was evaluating Kevin, and I remember finding my way back to the waiting room. Fear had gotten the best of me. I needed to catch my breath and allow the medical team to get things under control. It wasn't too long until the doctor got Kevin settled in a hospital room and told me that Kevin was very lucky. He said that this could have turned out much worse. The plan was to keep Kevin in the hospital for a few days to monitor him. I didn't leave the hospital the whole time Kevin was there. I made myself a comfy little space to sleep in the waiting room until Kevin was discharged. Looking back, it was a dress rehearsal for what was to come, but with a less happy ending.

Once Kevin arrived home from the hospital, we were given strict instructions that he was not to lift anything heavy and to rest and heal. I'm not sure that he listened 100%, as we were in the middle of a big move, but he complied well enough that he healed with no residual effects from the accident and bounced back to his strong, healthy self. The troops all came to our rescue and helped us with the big move.

Before I knew it, we had closed on our starter home, had moved into our new house in my hometown, and Kevin was healing better than we could ever have hoped. Kevin's angels were definitely watching out for him, and life couldn't be better.

It was now time to bless this house with a baby. Kevin and I had been trying to a certain extent, with no success, but you know the old saying, "New house, New baby." I was certain it was only a matter of a few months before I would be pregnant with our first child. So much to be grateful for and to look forward to.

Months passed, and we were still not pregnant. We followed the step-by-step instructions: record menstrual cycle frequency, monitor ovulation, and sex every other day during the fertile window. Yet month after month, we were unsuccessful. We saw several doctors to help us figure out what the problem might be. This led us to an infertility specialist. We went through the normal protocol of medications and procedures to improve the chances of conceiving. Nothing worked. We were now faced with what appeared to be the final option: In Vitro Fertilization, aka IVF. Sign me up! Kevin, on the other hand, had some reservations.

Although he wanted kids just as much as I did, Kevin felt maybe this was God's way of telling us that we weren't meant to have them. I didn't agree at all. We let the difference of opinion rest and figured we would revisit it at another time. I decided that the time to pick up this extremely important discussion was on a Saturday morning at the IHOP. Kevin loved the pancakes at IHOP. We went there often. A few days earlier, a really important story had been shared with me, and I decided to share it with Kevin during breakfast to hopefully change his mind about God's plan. The story went like this:

A man was trapped in his house during a flood. He began praying to God to rescue him. The water started to rise in his house. A park ranger urged him to leave and offered him a ride to safety. The man yelled back, "I am waiting for God to save me." The park ranger then drove off in his truck.

The man continued to pray and hold on to his vision. As the water began rising in his house, he had to climb to the second floor. A boat came by with some people heading for safe ground. They yelled at the man to climb through the window and that they would take him to safety. He told them that he was waiting for God to save him.

The man continued to pray, believing with all his heart that he would be saved by God. The floodwaters continued to rise. The man was forced to move to the roof, so he didn't drown.

A helicopter flew by, and a voice came over a loudspeaker, offering to lower a ladder and take him off the roof. The man waved the helicopter away, shouting back that he was waiting for God to save him.

The flooding water came over the roof and swept him away. He drowned.

When he reached heaven and asked, "God, why didn't you save me? I believed in you with all my heart. Why did you let me drown?" God replied, "I sent you a truck, a boat, and a helicopter."

I said to Kevin, "God sent us IVF." That was it. The story completely resonated with Kevin, and the decision was made. We were moving forward with IVF, and we both felt really good about it. This was a win, for sure. And the pancakes were super yummy! My stomach was full, and more importantly, my heart was too.

 Stay open to differing perspectives. One of life's greatest joys might be on the other side of another viewpoint.

T W O

F A I T H

It was game day. Three embryos were healthy and ready to be implanted. This was such an exciting and scary day. This was expensive, and our health insurance only paid for a small portion of the cost. The embryo transfer was a success, and now we had to wait. If there is one thing you should know about me, I am not a good waiter. Kevin had great patience, but I... not so much. Days felt like years waiting for that call from the doctor's office to let us know if we were pregnant. Although I am not patient, I am an eternal optimist. I was sure it would be successful. I knew we were meant to be parents. How could this not work? We put so much of our heart and soul into this process. There just had to be a happy ending on this pregnancy journey. Remember, IVF was the last option we had to have our own biological child. There were a lot of eggs in the IVF basket (no pun intended).

The phone call finally came. I knew that what was on the other side of this connection was either going to be the greatest news ever or the saddest. I knew it before my trembling hand picked up the phone. I know you know those kinds of moments. You have probably experienced it in your own life at least once. "I'm so sorry, Laurice. The procedure was not successful. You didn't get pregnant."

We were devastated. Disappointed. Defeated. A great deal of hope, time, energy, and effort went into IVF failure. And the expense. But we are definitely doing it again, I thought, "I don't care if I have to work three jobs," I cried. As I'm writing this and thinking back to that past version of me, my heart aches, and I have an intense desire to wrap my arms around my younger self and tell her that everything will be ok.

Time passed, and we met with the infertility specialists who shared with us that there is a lot of learning from the IVF failure to help increase our chances of getting pregnant in round two. We were told that they wanted to perform a laparoscopy (a surgical procedure used to treat endometriosis, which they believed the cause of our failed IVF). I remember feeling uplifted and frustrated all at once. I was encouraged that they believed they knew the reason I didn't get pregnant and had a way of fixing it. But at the same time, this meant months before I even had a chance of getting pregnant. At this point, months felt like an eternity. I'm not sure why. I just remember that's how it felt. *Remember, I'm not a good waiter.*

It was the day of the laparoscopy. I don't have a clear memory of the whole day, but I do remember waking up feeling groggy. The surgery was over. Our infertility specialist said to me, "the procedure went well. I will get you pregnant." Those words, "I will get you pregnant!" felt like someone had breathed a new life into my existence. Who knew that a long, thin viewing instrument inserted into my abdomen would produce those five magical words, "I will get you pregnant!!! Woohoo!! We were thrilled.

Take Two

The day was finally here, and so were four healthy embryos ready to be placed in my uterus. Yes, four! I didn't even question it because I didn't think we would be able to afford round three, and we all wanted to increase the chances of at least one embryo surviving. After all, in the last round, they had transferred three, and none of them had resulted in pregnancy. The transfer went well, and once again, the waiting game began. The awful, horrible, dreadful waiting game. *Do I need to remind you one more time that I am the worst waiter?*

The waiting was finally over, and so was the infertility journey. We were pregnant!! The nurse shared with me during our phone conversation that they all wanted to be the one to call and give us the amazing news. By this time, we were a regular at their office and had clearly won their hearts. Such kind, loving, and wonderful people. They were so happy for us. All that effort. All those negative pregnancy tests. All the tears. Finally, we are pregnant and starting the family that we dreamed about for so long.

Ohhhhh, keep reading; God has such a funny sense of humor...

At a routine visit, we were made aware of my high beta-hCG (human chorionic gonadotropin) levels, a hormone produced during pregnancy to support fetal growth. We were told that an elevated number could mean a multiple pregnancy. Of course, we knew this was a possibility when they transferred four embryos. We weren't really thinking anything much except that we were just so excited that we were pregnant and maybe, for me, a little tinge of "imagine if it was twins" thinking, solely because of these high hCG numbers. Bottom line - we were happy that we were pregnant and that things were moving along in the right direction.

Fast forward a few weeks, and we were at our first ultrasound. It's usually done at 7-8 weeks, but because we were high-risk, we may have had our first ultrasound appointment sooner. Kevin and I were at the appointment together. Not really sure what either of us was thinking at this point, but the time had arrived to definitively know the occupancy rate of my uterus. The technician put gel on the handheld wand called a transducer and moved it all around my belly. Seconds dragged by. We were not pregnant with one baby, not two babies, but three babies. Triplets!! I was scared and excited all at once. Glennon Doyle calls it scited!! That's the perfect word. I think I can speak for Kevin feeling scited too. Who would have ever thought three months ago that in thirtyish weeks we would be an instant family of five. Wow! A lot to take in and a lot to think about. I do remember, on our way to that appointment, discussing renovating a bathroom as our next project in our home. After the shock and excitement from the technician sharing that she found three heartbeats and we were having triplets, my husband announced from the side of his mouth, I don't think we're renovating the bathroom, lol!!!

Calling all high-risk pregnancy doctors! This was serious, and we wanted to do everything to increase our chances of carrying these babies as long as possible. We found a doctor who is affiliated with an excellent hospital not too far from our home. He came highly recommended by a family member, who was a nurse. We had a lot of confidence in him and felt "all" of us were in good hands under his care. He warned me that at 20 weeks, he would be putting me on strict bed rest. I would be allowed a shower every other day. I don't recall loving bedrest, and I have to tell you that today, in my current life, it sounds not only lovely but also luxurious!

Our third ultrasound appointment quickly approached, and it was week 12 of my pregnancy. At this point, one would think that nothing could surprise us - we're finally pregnant! With triplets! I can't imagine any more possible surprises. We wanted to know the sexes. I was going to be on bed rest at 20 weeks, and we needed to prepare. I don't know why but the possible combinations in my head were limited to two girls and a boy or two boys and a girl. I guess I assumed that from an odds standpoint, that was the most likely outcome. Surprise!!!

The room was quiet when the technician swirled the transducer around my belly a few times and finally got to a place where she saw something. Now, with intense concentration, she stared at the screen. She quickly announced, "Baby A is a boy!" Yay! A boy. My husband and I were gleaming with excitement. We were having a boy. Before I had a moment to soak it in, she shouted with a smile, "Baby B is another boy!" I could immediately see the excitement on my sports-loving husband's face - my double-play combination in baseball. My quarterback and receiver on the football field. He was thrilled. We both were. Of course, we were. We were finally pregnant!! At this point, if I'm being totally transparent, the realization hit me a little hard that we might not be having a boy(s) and girl pregnancy or a girl(s) and boy pregnancy. What?? Okay, here she goes. The final announcement and, at the time, what I was assuming would be my entire family. "Baby C," the technician shouted with excitement, "is another boy!" Triplet boys!! Holy testosterone! This was shocking to me. Don't get me wrong. I am so beyond grateful, just surprised. I probably shouldn't be - duh! They transferred four embryos. Why would I be surprised by triplets? I don't have a great answer. Perhaps because getting pregnant at all was so far out of our reach for many years that it all seemed shocking. Every bit of it. And all the same sex -

why was that such a surprise? No good answer there either. Just thought it would be some combination of boys and girls - Surprise!

 Dreams do come true. Sometimes they are bigger and better than you could have ever imagined. Don't give up. Stay committed to everything that you desire. Practice faith.

THREE

BELIEVE

The boys were born on December 11, 2000. They were six weeks early. Not bad for a multiple pregnancy. I was hospitalized for the last two weeks of the pregnancy. I'm not sure if the boys were ready, but I sure was! Before getting down to the final weeks of the pregnancy, Kevin and I had decided on the names. Baby A was to be Kelly, Baby B was to be Quinn, and Baby C was to be Tyler. A team of three nurses per baby were in the delivery room, my high-risk doctor, a few members of his medical team, and of course, my rock star husband Kevin (it was a big room!)

Frank Sinatra was playing softly in the background (on CD, he wasn't another person in the delivery room - although that would have been really cool!) Everyone was so excited to welcome these three little people into the world. Three healthy boys were born one minute apart. My doctor was very pleased with their weights and the length of time that I was able to carry them. Unfortunately, I was not doing as well as the babies. My blood pressure was very high, and I was pretty sick. I remained in the hospital for five additional days until I was well enough to go home. While I was recovering, Kevin was either by my side or with the babies in the neonatal intensive care unit. He officially named the babies. Baby A became Kelly, as planned. But Kevin switched the names for Baby B and Baby C, and the reason was adorable. At only 3 lbs 6 oz, Baby C was the smallest and had the most fighting to do. Manfred Mann had a song called "The Mighty Quinn." Our smallest baby, weighing only a little more than a half-gallon of milk, would need all his might to get bigger and stronger - he was our Mighty Quinn! Of course, now I cannot imagine the names being any other way.

The babies were released from the Hospital one at a time. Just after New Year's Day, all three of the boys were home. My parents moved in with us to help with round-the-clock care for the babies, returning home only on occasional weekends. Family and friends came daily as well as volunteers from some local churches and our hometown. My mother called our church to see if she could have something put in the bulletin about our unique situation and the need for some extra hands. When asked what she would like written in the bulletin, my mother responded, "HELP!" We would often laugh about that years later.

I was running a residential and commercial cleaning service from my home, and Kevin returned to work. It was time to begin a life as a family of five with lots of helpers passing through - some staying the night to help with the early morning feedings. I am still so thankful to everyone who so unselfishly filled our home with so much of their time, kindness, and love.

The first few months flew by, and the babies were getting a little bigger and stronger. The town nurse would stop by periodically to check on their progress. By the time they were almost a year old, the house had quieted down a bit. We had a pretty good routine. A good portion of the volunteers had dwindled down, and my parents moved back to their home. They visited often. A few of the volunteers still came each week to play with the babies and give us some free time to take care of other responsibilities. Occasionally, family or friends would stay over on the weekend to give us a break or a much-needed night out. One volunteer visited the boys on a weekly basis until they were five years old. So amazing. To help give Kevin and me some time alone, we created a quarterly Godparents weekend. Sort of our own made-up holiday that occurred not annually like ALL holidays but four times a year. So many advantages to a made-up holiday! Each child would visit their godparents for an overnight, and Kevin and I would have some free time to spend together quietly in our own house or out for a fun night. The big bonus was always getting to sleep the next morning. Nothing could beat the joy of going to bed knowing you could wake up slowly and at your leisure. It was so appreciated and so needed all at the same time. Sleep deprivation causes you to get very creative! Such amazing Godparents to embrace this made-up day of observance.

Although the first one to two years after the baby's arrival into this world are somewhat of a blur, I often remind myself of all that was given to us. Not only three beautiful, healthy babies who were thriving, but also a houseful of very kind, gentle, and giving people. Gratitude is an understatement. I hold a special place in my heart for every single person who joined Team Duffy and helped our family. At the one-year mark, we hosted a volunteer party for all of our amazing helpers. There was so much to celebrate.

I often reflect on the beautiful lesson to trust that God, the Universe, angels (whatever it is for you) have a far greater plan for each of us. My desire was to get pregnant with one child. The universe had much bigger plans for me. Let go of the way you think it should be and have faith in the spiritual realm and know that it is working on your behalf. Maintain faith even when it feels like it might not happen. Trust. Believe.

What if none of it is happening to you but rather happening for you?

Read that again. Let it sink in. Feel it in your body.

What if the most painful events of your life happened to redirect you toward your purpose?

How does that shift in perspective change your outlook?

Think about it...

FOUR

CHERISH

Having a large family was our dream but clearly not the dream for everyone who we came in contact with. This became evident from the unkind looks and remarks when people would walk by or meet me for the first time as I held the hands of my two-year-old triplets and so clearly had a baby on the way. Yes! Another surprise! We were just full of them, weren't we? We were pregnant again, and this time it was all on our own. No IVF or help from any doctors. I called this baby, who we would name Aidan, our bonus. We were thrilled. Not everyone shared in our excitement. At least not strangers, and in some cases, they made it known.

One memory, in particular, was when I was visiting Van Saun Park in Paramus, NJ, with my family. I was seven months pregnant and walking through the zoo there. People were more astounded by my presence (a pregnant woman with three 2-year-olds) than any animal they had at that zoo!

Others, I recall, were complete strangers being unnecessarily unkind - some comments that I remember, include:

Are you crazy?

Three boys, and you want another one?

Better you than me!

Are you going for the girl? I bet you want a girl!

All those boys - Oh my God!

I'm sure there were more that I probably blocked from my conscious mind. The ones that I mentioned are the ones that stand out. Yikes! People just say whatever the heck they want.

At times, it seemed as though shopping or going to restaurants as a family was judgment time. I often wondered why these people who didn't know anything about us felt that they had the right to ask personal questions, make snide remarks, or throw looks of disbelief at Kevin and me. I always wished that I was better prepared with a clever response. I never was.

I would tell myself that maybe these outspoken strangers were people who were unable to have children of their own, and seeing my large family made them sad and filled with envy. Another story I told myself was that some of them had terribly misbehaved children, and their comments were just pent-up frustration. None of it was probably true, but it made me feel better.

Speaking of frustration, trying to get four boys under the age of 5 to bed at night was no easy task. Besides it being the end of the day and feeling exhausted, the most challenging task of the day lay ahead - getting everyone settled in bed. I guess it's fair to say that getting them "IN" bed was fairly easy. It was the rigorous task of "KEEPING" them in bed that was difficult and took a large amount of patience. Patience that we, unfortunately, didn't always have by the end of the day. I used to describe bedtime as the Whack a Mole game that you would play on the boardwalk at the Jersey Shore. The objective of this high-energy, competitive game was as each mole quickly and randomly popped up; the contestant's job was to force the mole back into its mole hole by hitting it with a mallet. The children were the moles, Kevin and I were the (tired) contestants, and their beds were the holes. Oh yeah, and high energy was nothing that my husband and I even closely possessed by this time of the evening. I assure you that we did not have a mallet, lol! One child would be put to bed, blankets pulled up, a kiss/hug, and an I love you. One down! The second child was a repeat of the first, and we're close to doing an endzone dance. As soon as the third one was complete, "bing" the first or second one popped up. This could continue for what seemed like forever some nights. Not easy, but a phase. One of many phases. Usually, by the time we figured it out, the phase would change. I realized the only constant in life is change. Rolling with it with as much ease as possible was our best defense. Oh yeah, and as my wise mother always reminded me, a good sense of humor. She always reminded me that when raising kids, a good sense of humor was mandatory. She was so right.

The boys were getting older, and we were all feeling fairly comfortable in our roles as a family of six. Life was running pretty smoothly, for life, anyway. Of course, there were the normal hiccups that occur in families. Some of which included trips to the hospital for stitches, a banged-up bike, and child because he forgot that the brakes on his new bike were on the handlebars, not the pedals, and the only way to stop was to run into the garage refrigerator; an appendix surgery while on vacation; the realization that stress tests should no longer be taken at doctor's offices but at the home of 3rd-grade triplets while helping them complete homework. A true stress test! Oh yeah and playing the board game Hi Ho Cherry Oh. I'm certain there must still be some plastic cherries lodged in a baseboard or two in our house. Then, of course, as they got a little older, remembering whose turn it was to sit in the front seat. This was apparently very important and a big deal. Oh, right, and the time that I forgot one of them at the baseball field. I thought everyone was in the car. Full disclosure:

I probably wasn't paying complete attention as I began thinking about the five next things that had to happen before bedtime.

Halfway home, I shouted, "where's Aidan?" Everyone said. "I don't know." Quick U-turn and back to the field. There he was in the parking lot. That was a proud mama moment for sure!

I could go on, but I'm sure you can imagine and relate as you have probably experienced some of the exact same moments in your own home raising children.

There were also beautiful moments. Memories that will forever be imprinted on my soul. I recall one memory in particular that always makes me smile. I'm truly grateful that it's mine to keep forever.

The older boys were in their early teens. They all played baseball for Triboro. This was a team made up of three towns in our area. They were a very good team filled with competitive athletes and childhood friendships. Kevin and I loved watching them play.

At the end of each year, the coaches picked an All-Star roster. This was a team consisting of eleven or twelve of the best-performing players from all Triboro teams. They played other All-Star teams from surrounding towns – it was a one-game loss elimination until a champion team won the whole tournament. The players that didn't make the All-Star team were combined and played in a consolation game which was basically an end-of-the-year game played for fun.

We had three boys on this team, and only two made the All-Star team. Of course, we felt bad for our one son who didn't make it, but we knew the selection was fair. Our son was disappointed but very accepting and understanding of the choices made as he, too, knew it was fair. The other two boys were very thoughtful of his feelings and didn't make a big deal about it in front of him. As their parents, we tried hard to balance our excitement for the two boys who made it with concern for our other son's feelings. Sometimes it felt tricky, but we worked hard on trying to get it right.

It was game day. The All-Star game was being played on this particular day, and so was the consolation game. Same day. Same time. Different fields. Ugh!!!

My husband arrived home from work moving quickly, as he always did when the boys had any type of sporting event or were participating in anything. He never wanted to miss watching them in anything that they were part of. Often, he was their coach, but if he wasn't coaching them, he rushed home anyway to make sure he could watch them and not miss a minute of whatever it was that they were involved in. He got in and out of the shower in record time and proceeded to get dressed for the game. While he was getting ready, I made a comment implying that we were going to the All-Star game. He said to me, "No. No, I'm not going to the All-Star game. I'm going to the consolation game. I would never send the message that that game, and watching him play in it, was any less important than the other boys' game. He mattered, and I was going to make sure that he knew it." I was struck by pure love and amazement. I said, "Of course. Of course, that's where we're going." It was at that moment that I was so clearly reminded of the beautiful human being that I chose to be my husband and the father of our four children. Wow!

Let me share with you that Kevin loved a good game. He loved watching competitive sports and talented athletes. That wasn't what this was about, and he didn't allow it to muddy his decision of which game to attend. This was an opportunity to make sure that it was crystal clear that he wasn't any more proud of the other boys because they made the All-Star team than he was of this child who didn't.

 This was such a beautiful opportunity to demonstrate that his love and attention were not conditional - not performance or achievement focused but rather unconditional, cherished love. This was about a relationship, not results, and he was going to make sure that his presence at that consolation game sent that message home. It could have been such an easy miss. But it wasn't missed. It was embraced.

All four boys shared in Kevin's love of sports. The five of them watched and attended sporting events together. Kevin coached their teams, and they played together in the front yard. Kevin was always the steady QB. He taught them to be mentally tough and compete hard. When Kevin was their coach, if a player was struggling, he knew how to take a beat and calm him down with a joke or a kind word. Unless it was one of his sons, in which case he would say something like, "Could you please throw a damn strike!?!" or "You're allowed to play defense in this game!" We often chuckled about that.

Kevin instilled in the boys kindness, manners, respect, a love for the Boston Red Sox, and a heartfelt hatred for the New York Yankees. So much so that when the boys played on a

Yankee Triboro baseball team, they were playfully told by their father to leave their Yankee hats in the shed. Sorry, Yankee fans!

He was an extraordinary man with a great deal of love for his family. He was a hard worker and a fierce competitor. Even his rendition of "Teenager in Love" was one of the best Karaoke performances of all time. He thought so, anyway, lol!

The owner of his favorite deli summed it up best when Kevin walked in and ordered a coffee with milk and sugar. Repeating the order, the owner yelled back, "Regular coffee for a regular guy!" That's who Kevin was. A regular but extraordinary guy who gracefully touched many lives. And he was my husband and my children's dad. So beyond blessed. We were living the American dream. For now, anyway.

FIVE

NUDGE

It was a typical weekday. Kevin's eyes snapped open before his alarm from another restless night's sleep. He was never a good sleeper. He put on his work clothes and sat in the same chair in the corner of our bedroom and laced up his work boots. It was still dark outside. I was usually sleeping or at least barely awake and snuggled under the covers while he scurried around the room, attempting to be as quiet as possible. He kissed me goodbye. He never left for work without kissing me goodbye. Unless, of course, we had an argument, then he may have skipped the kiss in an attempt to send the message that he was still upset. Silly arguments that were about nothing except for two people who wanted to feel understood. How I would respond so differently today. Anyway, off to work he went. Kevin was a union pipefitter and had gone through a 5-year apprenticeship before becoming a journeyman. He was a hard worker, often promoted to foreman in the different companies he worked for through the years. His work ethic and punctuality were admirable. He knew how to mix hard work with fun. He could make a game or a challenge out of anything.

The boys woke up for school at the very last minute possible. They would shower, brush their teeth, and race out the door. This was how every morning went on a school day. They somehow managed to stay asleep until the final second. They knew just when they needed to jump out of bed in order to get to school within seconds of the late bell ringing. They had perfected the art of getting themselves together in record time without a tardy... usually.

The house was quiet. Everyone had gotten to where they needed to be for the day. I loved weekdays for this reason. It was an opportunity to be home alone. Listen to the sweet sound of silence. Soak in the calm. Hear myself think without interruption. Relax in the beauty of organization. But this day was different. On this particular day, I felt uneasy and restless. I couldn't put my finger on it, but I knew something wasn't right. The phone rang. It was a close girlfriend. She could tell I didn't sound like my normal self and asked me if everything was ok. This was my response:

I married the love of my life and a man who adores me. We have four amazing, healthy children after years of infertility, we live in a nice home in a desirable area, my parents and extended family are supportive, wonderful people, I am blessed with great friends, I get to run my business from home (at that time I owned a commercial and residential cleaning business) and be home for my kids - Don't you think that I should be skipping around the house? Because I'm not. I want more.

We chatted about it. There was no resolution. No big aha. How could someone else understand me when I could barely understand myself? We hung up the phone. Instead of relief, I found myself drowning in disbelief that I could be so selfish. *So ungrateful. People would give their right arm to have what I have,* I thought, *and I want more!*

I had been having these feelings for quite a while but to speak them out loud made them feel so real. Almost as if the activity of speaking my feelings instead of just thinking about them made them true. So, there I sat, almost resenting the quiet of everyone's absence which I normally love because it was forcing me to be with these uncomfortable feelings. Nothing had changed except the added load of shame and self-judgment. I ignored the nudge. It didn't go away. I just decided to convince myself that this was enough. That this should be enough and needed to be enough. I shouldn't want too much. Nice girls are happy with what they have (what a load of crap that is!). I think my internal dialogue was probably on repeat, saying something like, "You want more? How about I take away some of the amazing things in your life. Then you'll learn to appreciate what you have." You may relate. You may have felt like this at some point in your own life. You may feel like this now.

I pushed it down untended and, like a bandage, placed thoughts of gratitude over my discontent feelings, and hoped it would heal seamlessly like a deep opening of the skin. Shame and guilt overpowered my mind and took away the opportunity to get quiet, curious, and listen to the whisper of my soul. Desires that had been so purposefully placed in my heart for a reason. How did something that now feels so beautiful identify as so complex and indecent? Why was I more committed to dismissing a feeling rather than following the nudge? We don't know what we don't know. The good news is that once we know it, we can never unknow it. Unfortunately, at that point in my life (about 45 years old), I didn't know and chose to bury it rather than address the idea that maybe it had nothing at all to do with not being grateful enough and everything to do with being meant for more.

I continued running my cleaning business. I had started it about two years after graduating college. I wasn't happy with my nine-to-five job and felt a bit stuck. I had a bachelor's degree in Psychology but didn't really know what to do with it. I had always wanted to work as a therapist, but that meant continuing my education, and at that time in my life, I wasn't interested in going back to school. I made the decision to start something on my own - become an entrepreneur. I loved the idea of a paycheck matching my effort rather than a predetermined salary before even starting. This was the answer. I know I could make a lot more money with my own business than with any office job that I might be qualified for. My thought process at that time in my life was about making money rather than finding fulfillment. I started out working as a solopreneur and slowly grew the business gaining more accounts. I was excited to get to the point where I needed to hire employees. I then expanded my residential cleaning company to commercial accounts too. In about four or five years, I had gotten it to the point that I was no longer working in the field and instead at home doing all the office work. I had about 4-6 part-time employees. My business helped pay some of the bills, which made me feel good and gave us a little more freedom. I liked dictating my own schedule and being my own boss. That served me well for quite a while until it didn't.

Life went on. We continued living our beautiful life, which was filled with everything from sporting events to backyard barbecues with family, friends, and various teams that the boys played on. Everything from rec leagues to travel and club teams. It was a lot of fun. Our kids kept us very busy, and Kevin's coaching schedule made us an even busier family. He loved it, and so did the kids. So many of the athletes that lived in our community also benefited from Kevin's love for the game, his great ability to coach, and his knack for making almost anything fun. They loved it when they were picked to be on Coach Duffy's team, and I believe a lot of the parents did too. He was fair while being firm and taught these kids so much more than just a game.

I felt so fortunate that my kids had such a great dad - one who loved and adored them so much but one who also understood the importance of instilling good qualities in them. He would always remind the boys to get up if we were at a restaurant waiting for a table and an elderly person walked in and needed a seat. He often had conversations with the boys about sticking up for the underdog and intervening if anyone was ever getting bullied. He felt passionate about kindness and had many discussions with the kids about the importance of doing the right thing. As a result, they have always gotten along well and treated each other with respect and high regard. Kevin was a good man, and he was committed to raising good men.

And there lay the nudge like an elephant in the room that I continued to overlook with the hope that one day it would miraculously disappear. Some days I was so busy that I didn't notice it. On other days I bumped into it with every move I made.

Our feelings don't go away when we push them down and refuse to acknowledge them. Imagine holding a beach ball in a pool and using all your might to hold it beneath the surface of the water. Every time you let go, it pops back up. It takes effort to hold that beach ball under the water. A lot of effort. Consider the beach ball your feelings - it takes a lot of strain to keep them pushed down. And remember, what we resist persists. No matter how far you push them down, they will always pop back up. Suppressing your emotions is a short-term fix - never a permanent solution. No matter what, remember this - in order to heal it, you need to feel it.

And when you're feeling it, please don't judge it. Nothing heals in judgment. Just allow it. Be with it. Get curious about it. And then let it go. 🎈

"Women believe that if we can imagine more, it's because we're not grateful enough- instead of considering that if we can imagine more, it might mean that we were made for more."

~ Glennon Doyle

S I X

HORROR

It was a summer night in 2014, and we were out for pizza with close friends. It was our first time at this particular restaurant. I love pizza, and I loved a fun night out with people that we both enjoyed. The older boys were now allowed to stay home together for a few hours without a babysitter—an added bonus. I remember feeling particularly relaxed and excited for an outing on this warm summer night. We were eating our dinner and enjoying a drink, laughing, and sharing stories. As the conversation continued and my girlfriend's husband excused himself to use the restroom, Kevin shared with us that he felt like he was talking strange. He told us that his tongue felt swollen, and he heard a slur when speaking. My friend and I hadn't noticed anything peculiar and thought his speech sounded the way it always did. Our friend told him that maybe he was allergic to the yeast in beer and had an allergic reaction. Although that seemed like a good possibility, it was odd that it was just starting now. He had certainly drunk beer before without any problems with his speech. We all dismissed it and thought it wasn't anything to get worried about. I honestly thought that it would probably go away just as oddly as it appeared. It didn't affect the mood or the fun energy we all brought that night. We had a great time and enjoyed the evening.

A week or two after that night out, Kevin made an appointment with our family doctor to have this very slight but disturbing slur checked out. At this point, I still couldn't hear it but realized that for Kevin to make an appointment with the doctor, he was definitely concerned. This initial appointment with our family doctor turned into a series of bloodwork, tests, and referrals to other doctors - all of whom were attempting to identify what was at the root of this odd slur and swollen tongue feeling. A few months passed, and we were still no further in our search for the cause of this irritating feeling of his tongue.

Kevin was now also experiencing leg cramps that were pretty severe. I don't remember thinking that there was a connection. We all thought he wasn't drinking enough water or perhaps was magnesium deficient. Maybe Kevin needed more potassium in his diet. I remember an especially bad cramp one night and my youngest son hearing Kevin moan. He quickly ran down the stairs into the kitchen and grabbed a banana. He hurried into our bedroom and handed Kevin the banana. I guess somewhere he heard us talking about a lack of potassium causing leg cramps and bananas being a good source of it. Moments like that I always found to be very funny. I think Kevin was even laughing in between the pain of the cramp. Again, not worried. You have to remember my husband was a very healthy, strong, and athletic guy. He didn't drink alcohol very often and didn't do drugs or smoke at all. He wasn't overweight or underweight. There was no doubt in my mind that these were minor issues that could be easily remedied or possibly still go away on their own.

It was March 2015. Kevin and I had reservations for dinner in Manhattan and tickets to the Broadway musical, Jersey Boys. Kevin was so excited. He loved singing and dancing and Broadway shows. He loved talent and being entertained. He had wanted to see this show for a long time. This was a night we were both looking forward to. We had a great dinner not too far from the theater. Getting our food took longer than expected. I remember noticing that we were starting to cut it close. We shared with our waitress that we had tickets for a show and hoped that our food would be out with enough time to eat it. Shortly thereafter, the food arrived. We were forced to eat it a little quicker than we would have ideally liked to, but that's how it goes sometimes. We quickly paid for our meal, and off we went. We realized that we were a little further away from the theater than we thought, and our rapid stride soon turned into a steady jog, uncomfortably and rudely weaving in and out of people. At some point towards the end of this ridiculous display of poor planning, I looked over at Kevin and noticed his one foot was dropping while we were still running. I said to him, "What is happening with your left side?" He replied with a gasp, trying to catch his breath from running after a heavy Italian meal, "I have no idea." This caught my attention.

We got to the show and were escorted to our seats. We quickly found ourselves engrossed in the beautiful scenery and talent before us, forgetting about the race to get there and this newly discovered symptom.

More doctors and still no answers. It was frustrating, but by this point, I was sure he'd been tested for all the scary diagnoses, and those were removed from the list of possibilities. The slight slur continued, and so did the leg cramps and sometimes the drop foot. We were still searching and knew that, eventually, we would figure it out.

In the meantime, life needed to go on. Kevin was approaching his 50th birthday and I wanted to do something special for this important milestone. I decided to plan a surprise all-inclusive trip for us to the Bahamas. I knew he would love this idea and be excited to get away. Due to the size of our family we were mindful with our budget, so I immediately removed the idea of bringing the kids, worried that it would get too expensive. Looking back, a big regret.

We left on a Tuesday and would return home on Saturday. I made arrangements with his boss and shared the surprise with Kevin a few days before we left. In my opinion, some of the fun is the anticipation of a vacation, so I wanted him to have some time to be excited about what was to come. I knew this was going to be exactly what we both needed – an enjoyable and relaxing time together without the worries of doctors, symptoms, and unanswered questions.

I remember so vividly landing at the airport and getting to the baggage claim. Kevin had to use the bathroom. Standing next to me was a family also waiting for their luggage. They had two small children with them. The little boy, probably a bit younger than my youngest son, was jumping and dancing around in excitement to be in the Bahamas. I was no longer watching out for our luggage but engrossed in this little boy's joy of being on this family vacation. A tear rolled down my eye. I felt an ache in my heart that I had robbed our children of so much happiness, excitement, and precious family time because of money. It was almost like my heart knew this would be the last trip. Kevin returned from the bathroom. I quickly wiped my face, never sharing my discontent in an attempt to not dampen the excitement of what was ahead.

Once at the hotel, the sky's bright blue palette appeared to go on for miles while the blazing sun shined so brilliantly. We laid on the white sandy beach and had cocktails by the pool.

We swam in the crystal clear, turquoise-blue ocean. I have a beautiful memory of Kevin lifting me up and out of the water. I wrapped my arms around his neck so tightly. A beautiful embrace of true love as beads of water slowly trickled down our fixed gaze. It was as if time had stopped at that moment, and for a split second, we both knew something that we actually didn't know at all.

It was late afternoon. We showered and dressed for dinner. By this time, there was a slight cool breeze in the air. Our sunburned skin was a reminder of our beautiful day at the beach. We ate at a restaurant overlooking the water. We were soaking in all the beauty that surrounded us. After dinner, we decided to go for a walk. It was during that stroll that Kevin noticed that he couldn't lift his heel. He looked up at me with fright in his eyes and asked if I thought it was possible, he was having a stroke. I assured him that he wasn't having a stroke and we would figure it out when we got back home. I reminded him that he recently had a whole series of tests done, and everything came back normal. I think his mind was temporarily put at ease. I do recall, however, getting back to our room and researching this new symptom. Although I was usually the calm, more relaxed one, I needed a little reassurance too. We read through some possibilities as we lay in our bed, and by the next morning, we put it behind us and chose to enjoy the rest of our trip. We knew we would see more doctors when we got home, and eventually, we would get to the bottom of all these peculiar things happening to Kevin.

The flight back home may go down as the worst travel day for me to date. I developed a little stomach bug the day before we left the island. I think I drank tap water at one of the restaurants. Total amateur move and a mistake I will never make again.

We arrived at the airport early and waited patiently at the gate until it was time to leave. My stomach was a bit queasy but tolerable. We were very excited to get home and see the kids. We bought them t-shirts and some fun little toys that we knew they would enjoy. We boarded the plane and proceeded to our seats. Kevin and I were in a row of three. Kevin was near the window, and I was in the middle seat. Shortly after we were settled, a woman walked up the aisle with her two children and husband trailing behind her. She sat next to me, and her husband and kids sat in the row adjacent to ours. She immediately whipped out hand sanitizer for her family and a Costco size container of disinfectant wipes for each of them to clean their trays, seats, arm rests and anything in their vicinity that may have a germ. I remember thinking how ironic it was that she was sitting next to the lady with a queasy stomach. If she only had known, she probably would have wiped me down with one of her disinfectant wipes. She certainly would have changed seats. I thought I would be fine, and for almost the whole trip, I was. It was right before landing. You know the time of the flight that you must fasten your seatbelts and remain in your seats no matter what? Yeah. You know what's coming. We began to experience some turbulence, and my stomach lost its ability to keep everything under control. Kevin quickly grabbed the handy little paper bag they conveniently supplied in the pouch in front of you. I proceeded to get sick as Kevin so kindly rubbed my head and reminded me that I would be ok. He was so loving and caring. Not bothered at all that I only had this tiny bag to use as my container. He just felt bad for me and the discomfort that I was experiencing. The woman next to me, on the other hand, pushed herself as far away as her seat belt would allow. Not that I blame her. I get it, but here is the part I didn't understand. She never offered me any of her disinfectant wipes. We surely could have used one. She had a very large tub! She grabbed her kids and bolted off that plane. I laughed, thinking about her sharing the story with friends. I wouldn't have wanted to sit next to me that day either, but what are the chances of someone with excessive germ concerns being the lucky winner? Ha!

In the car, I was tired and worried that my stomach wouldn't make the car ride home from the airport. I remember talking myself through, "Ok, just get me to the car. Ok just get me to Rt. 24. Ok, just get me to 287....." Finally, we made it home. My shower and bed were only a few short steps away. *Thank you, dear God,* I thought to myself.

Kevin grabbed our luggage from the car and followed me into the house. Immediately I see my sister and brother-in-law sitting at the kitchen counter - ALL. DRESSED. UP. I didn't even have time to think before my eyes widened and the words spit out of my mouth, "What have you done?" "SURPRISE," they yelled. "Your guests will be here in about 30 minutes. We're having a 50th birthday party for Kevin!" Oh my gosh! I wanted to cry. It was so kind and incredibly thoughtful, but I did not feel good, and now I had to make it through a party! I was so close to being in my pajamas, in bed, with a hot water bottle on my stomach and a cup of tea. Instead, I needed to put on a nice outfit, a smile, and make pleasant conversation. Ugh!! I dawdled to my bedroom, mumbling, "I can't believe this. I cannot believe this is happening." I sat on my bed for a moment, but I didn't dare let my head hit the pillow. I knew this pause needed to be short-lived. I showered, got dressed, and reminded myself that I could get through a few more hours. I then would be able to lay in my bed and rest for as long as I needed. "You can do this, Laurice," I cheered to myself.

The party was great. I think Kevin had a really nice time. The kids were there too, and all gave a little speech that they wrote for their dad. It was so sweet. The food that had been prepared looked delicious. I, however, didn't dare eat a thing. Our last guest left somewhere around 11 o'clock that evening. The house was all cleaned up by family and friends, and after a very long day, Kevin and I went to bed. We were fast asleep within minutes of our heads hitting the pillow.

Somehow vacation creates this mystical illusion where reality very quietly lingers away as beautifully as the water wisps back into the never-ending ocean. And then, one morning, your eyes open, and the reality of real life hits you hard. It's definitely a sobering moment. I was grateful for an easy Sunday of leisure and relaxation. Fortunately, my stomach was starting to feel better by the afternoon.

But now it was Monday, and we must address Kevin's new symptom and continue on our search for a diagnosis. Kevin's primary physician suggested he see a neurologist as the next best step. I had a neurologist that I had been seeing due to migraines. Kevin made the appointment and went to see him after work one day. This doctor examined Kevin and recommended he see a neurologist specialist. He gave him the name of someone that he knew and trusted. Kevin made the appointment for a weekday at 10 am. I remember that day like it was yesterday. Kevin had taken the day off from work, and we were excited to spend the day together and go out to lunch afterward.

The morning of the appointment arrived, and we were both in a good mood. Kevin had the whole day off, which made having an early appointment especially nice. In the waiting room, Kevin and I were kidding around and joking with each other. The mood was very light. It wasn't long before we were both called into the doctor's office. The doctor examined Kevin and did an electromyogram (EMG), a test that evaluates the electrical activity of muscles when they contract and when they're at rest. Kevin was getting a lot of leg cramps, so this seemed appropriate. The doctor completed the exam, sat us down, and with a concerned expression, stated, "this is very serious." He quickly got my attention. I felt an immediate increase in my heart rate as well as that feeling of high alert. We had no idea what was coming next. I can still feel the doctor's words wrap around my neck as I gasped for air. He told us that he was pretty sure Kevin was in the beginning stages of Amyotrophic Lateral Sclerosis, or ALS. Kevin asked what that meant exactly. We knew about the "Ice Bucket Challenge", but we weren't too sure what it meant to have an ALS diagnosis. His exact words, "how much do you want to know?" My heart rate sped up, and now I felt like I was going to be sick. Kevin quickly responded, "we want to know everything." The doctor told us that ALS is a progressive neurodegenerative disease that affects nerve cells in the brain and spinal cord. He explained that the illness would most likely affect Kevin's walking, arm movements, speech, swallowing, and breathing. He told us there is no cure for this disease and that the average survival time is 3 to 5 years. I don't have words to properly express my horror. Terror darted through my veins at a very rapid speed.

For weeks, it was difficult to eat, sleep or get out of my pajamas. I was fully consumed with grief, fear, and disbelief. It was hard to function, yet we had to as we made the decision not to tell the kids until the original diagnosis was confirmed with a second opinion. We made an appointment at the Neuromuscular & ALS Center of New Jersey at the Rutgers Robert Wood Johnson Medical School in New Brunswick. I was feeling so nervous and praying that this doctor would give us some better news. Anything. Anything but a terminal illness.

I remember so clearly when this doctor confirmed the ALS diagnosis. The doctor was very confident and matter-of-fact about his findings. For him, this was routine, his job. For Kevin, this was his life. For me, this was my beautiful husband and the father of our four children who needed their dad. I couldn't believe that this was our reality. I couldn't imagine anything worse, and then it hit me, something worse - we now had to go home and share the horrific news with our kids. I didn't think my heart was capable of feeling more pain.

I remember coming home and calling all the kids into the family room. They were nervously asking, "what's going on?" as, one by one, they entered the room. We all sat down. The boys looked concerned and uneasy. By this point they were suspicious and recognized that something was out of the ordinary. I always think I'm convincing, but kids know when something is wrong. We shared what we had been told as delicately as possible "Dad has ALS." They didn't know a lot about it except the most devastating part, that there was no cure. We went on to remind them that Duffy's don't give up (a family mantra) and that daddy was a fighter. We assured them that although we couldn't guarantee the outcome, we would be doing everything in our power to get him well and that we were already looking into clinical trials for ALS that daddy might be a candidate for. I also promised them that we would truthfully share everything with them as it was told to us. One of my most unforgettable memories of that day was later on that evening when everyone went to bed. My youngest son came into my room overwhelmed with emotion from the pain of what was and the uncertainty of what would come. I took his hand, and together, we walked back to his room. I crawled into bed with him wrapping my arms around his body as tight as I possibly could. The back of his head tucked gently under my chin. He said to me, in this order,

"How will we get daddy's wheelchair up the stairs?

When will daddy die?

How will you be able to afford for us to live here?

I don't ever want you to have a boyfriend."

Oh, this poor baby, that's a lot, I thought. His little mind had gone to places that mine hadn't yet traveled. My heart was broken for so many reasons. I told him that we were surrounded by a lot of strength, support and love. I assured him that it would all get worked out and he didn't need to worry about any of it. In that moment, I held him even tighter - my way of making him feel safe in a reality that left me feeling everything but...

 Such a profound moment of clarity as to the depth and wholeness of a *mother's* love even when she is broken.

SEVEN

CHASE

After a few weeks of friends and family providing strength and support, we learned about Lyme disease and that many of the symptoms overlapped with ALS. At first, Kevin and I felt like we needed to accept the diagnosis now given to us by two different doctors. But then a family friend sent us an email sharing the name of a LLMD (Lyme literate medical doctor) who had discovered a misdiagnosis of multiple sclerosis (MS) in someone she knew. Both ALS and MS are neurodegenerative diseases that affect the brain, and spinal cord and although MS is not terminal, neither illness has a cure. This particular doctor treated her for Lyme disease, and in the end, her symptoms and her diagnosis of MS were resolved. This was hope. We had nothing else. At the very least, we had nothing to lose in making an appointment. We visited the specialist, and he examined Kevin and did some non-conventional testing on him. He quickly believed that Kevin had been misdiagnosed and had Lyme disease. Of course, Lyme disease testing is unreliable, and there isn't a test that can give you a definitive diagnosis for ALS, but this doctor seemed pretty certain, and we were feeling a glimmer of hope. This was better news than anything we had received thus far. I began reading everything I could get my hands on about Lyme disease. A close friend even found a story online about a man, Dr. Dave Martz. Dr. Martz was given the devastating diagnosis of ALS and only had two years to live. As his health took a turn for the worse, Martz found a Lyme disease specialist who prescribed a heavy cocktail of antibiotics. Within a year, he was well. The doctor who had given Dr. Martz the ALS diagnosis made his own determination that the ALS condition was completely gone. This was super encouraging. At this point I was pretty convinced that Kevin had been misdiagnosed with ALS and was fighting Lyme disease. Moments when Kevin felt less than hopeful, I read him articles, cheered him on, and convinced him that he was going to get well.

During this time, I found out about Life Coaching School. Remember the nudge? Well, you see, I have my bachelor's degree in psychology and always wanted to be a therapist or help people in some way, but I didn't have the desire to continue my education for two more years. Without a master's degree, this was an impossible goal. About a week went by after finding out about this Life Coaching profession, and my friend said to me, "Oh, I have been meaning to tell you that I met a woman whose daughter is on my daughter's volleyball team, and she's a Life Coach." I quickly shouted before she had time to continue, "I want to be a Life Coach!" She told me about the school that her new friend went to, and within a few weeks, I was signed up with iPEC, Institute for Professional Excellence in Coaching. It was the worst time in my life to be taking on another activity - I had four children, a sick husband, and a business to run. I wasn't sure how it was all going to work, but I knew I needed to do this. We are either pushed by pain or pulled by pleasure, and I was definitely being pushed by pain. When we were given the original diagnosis of ALS, I remember thinking at one point, *I am a mom and a wife. If my husband could pass away between 3-5 years, that would be exactly around the time that my three older boys will leave for college. Who will I be? Without the title of mom and wife, who am I?* That was an eye-opening moment of realizing that my identity wasn't tied to anything that couldn't leave or be taken away. The final decision to move forward was made after my son and I took a ride to visit my parents one night. While he was busy in another room, my parents and I quietly discussed my new idea to pursue this training. They were proud of me and even offered to support my new venture by paying for half the tuition cost. I was very grateful and saw this as a further sign that this was my destiny. I didn't want my son to hear our conversation in case I chose not to do it. I didn't want him to think that his mom would quit on her dreams, yet the truth was I wasn't sure I could handle everything I was juggling at that point. We said our goodbyes to my parents, and my son and I got in the car. Clearly, I'm not as a quiet as I think. He immediately said to me, "Mom, you might become a life coach? I think you should. Just the way you sit on the edge of my bed and give such great advice - you would be a really good life coach." That was it. I signed up the next day. I knew that if my son had so much confidence in me, I needed to, also.

Some days were better than others. We visited the same Lyme specialist once a month for close to a year. Kevin was on a standard prescription of antibiotics with no improvement. The doctor's office was an hour and a half away, and I hated going. The appointments caused me so much distress and anxiety. This doctor was the only hope we had, and at every appointment, I was petrified that it would get taken away. With that being said, each time the course of antibiotics was changed, we felt excited that maybe we would finally see some progress. Change meant possibility. Possibility meant hope. Unfortunately, after almost a year, there was never any progress. Not even a little bit. By this time, I had found another doctor. We decided to make an appointment with him and see if he agreed with the Lyme diagnosis and, if so, what plan of action he would put in place to get Kevin well. Another anxiety-filled ride. This time to Rhinebeck, NY. *What if he tells us that he doesn't think it's Lyme disease*, I thought to myself. I was scared to death. But we had to do something different. We needed to see some improvement. Anything to confirm that we were on the right track and that Kevin, my children's dad, was going to be ok. I wanted to scream with my anxiety-filled lungs, "Please, someone, save my children's dad!!" I never did. Instead, I let the fear and anxiety fill me up like an overblown balloon while I maintained a measure of stability that I knew my family so desperately needed. On the outside, I provided leadership and strength. On the inside, I was seething with desperation and terror.

Our new doctor agreed with the Lyme disease diagnosis and took a very aggressive approach to get Kevin well, which included therapies, intravenous antibiotics, and much more. After almost a year and a half with our new doctor and even more specialists, diets, BioMat, and any possible remedy we thought might be helpful, Kevin wasn't getting better. He was actually declining.

To make matters worse, Kevin's wonderful dad passed away. Many friends that hadn't seen Kevin for a while were at the funeral. Individually many shared the same thought - "This is not Lyme disease." How did I become so blind? My laser focus on how I wanted things to be caused my inability to see how they actually were. My kids were even more aware than I was by this point. They recognized the decline and knew their dad was not going to get better. How did they see it, but I didn't? It amazes me how sometimes pain can have the overwhelming ability to distort the truth. I couldn't hold on any longer. Denial is a heavy weight, and I was feeling exhausted and frail. I needed to have a very difficult conversation with myself and my now feeble husband when I asked if we were searching for answers or running from the truth. That was a hard day. A really hard day. I read somewhere that by finding and sharing what is genuine for you, you can clear a path for a person to come closer to their truth. How unsettling that the path I was clearing for the person I loved so much would lead to a dead end...literally.

It was time to get back in touch with the ALS community and see another specialist.

 "Don't forget every truth you tell is a kindness even if it makes people uncomfortable and every truth you don't tell is an unkindness even if it makes people comfortable."

~ Liz Gilbert

EIGHT

TRUTH

We went to Columbia Presbyterian Hospital in NY. Another anxiety-filled car ride. Fortunately, our very close friend drove us. She attended most appointments and was a huge comfort and support for me. The doctor we saw was Wesley J. Howe, Professor of Neurology at Columbia University at The Neurological Institute of New York and New York-Presbyterian Hospital/Columbia University Medical Center. This senior consultant examined Kevin as well as the medical records provided by the first two ALS specialists who diagnosed Kevin. I'll never forget my focus on this doctor's every facial expression praying for any glimpse of doubt or uncertainty about Kevin's condition and the original diagnosis His exact words to us were, "I don't know if you have Lyme disease or not. What I do know is that you have ALS." Another punch in the gut. We were exactly where we started from almost two years prior. A reminder that acceptance was my only choice.

This time I surrendered. I had no strength. I had no choice. Hope felt hopeless.

After leaving NY, we went straight home. It was time to talk to our four boys and remove the false hope we so innocently and irresponsibly placed in their hearts. We sat them down and shared the certainty of the news. "Dad does, in fact, have ALS." Everyone was quiet. The only words spoken were, "Mom, are you ok?" The question struck me as odd, almost insensitive. Why was I asked if I was ok and not their father? After all, he was the sick one. He was the one who was going to die.

I thought about those four words for days. They ran on repeat in my mind. And then I got it. I finally got it. You see, my kids weren't particularly surprised by the news. By this time, they had actually accepted the idea that their dad was declining (they were watching it), and they were probably going to lose him. What they needed to be sure of was that they weren't going to lose their mom too. Suddenly it seemed so clear. I didn't have control over Kevin's illness. I didn't have control over losing my husband or my kids losing their father. I never had control. Control was an illusion that I feverishly chased with no success until I was beaten down tired. But I did have control over something - ME! The power was within, and I had the power to choose. "Mom are you ok" became my superpower. The key that unlocked my strength. I couldn't change WHAT was happening to my family, but I had the power to choose WHO I would be while it was happening. At this point, it was clear that the best me I could be for my family was to embrace acceptance, be a leader, and with resolve, choose how we were going to move forward. I chose strength as I knew it would provide my family with stability. I chose to feel my pain as I knew it would provide my family permission to feel their own. I chose truth which so powerfully provided trust.

Steve Maraboli says it best, "Incredible change happens in your life when you decide to take control of what you do have power over instead of craving control over what you don't." I needed to begin taking control of the power that I had, and that was exactly what I did. I began to live by a coaching principle that I learned at iPEC:

Each moment describes

who you are, and

gives you the opportunity to decide

if that's who you want to be

I decided to live each day with intention. To *decide* who I was going to be. I quickly recognized that when life was amazing, I was a great Mom, wife, daughter, sister, friend, and aunt. That was easy. Who was I going to be when life was at rock bottom? That was a big question. I knew I got to choose.

At this point, the meaning of hope changed. Hope was now about navigating the reality of what was and what everyone needed in order to make the best out of the *truth.* This was difficult because Kevin still wanted hope. Of course, he did. I followed the advice of my priest when he told me, "Laurice, giving false hope is not only unkind but cruel." It was one of the hardest stages of this entire awful and gut-wrenching ordeal. I was no longer able to give my beautiful husband the one thing that he desperately wanted - Hope. I would have given him anything, but I knew at this point truth had to win over false hope. I didn't listen to the voice of my inner knowing when I thought we needed to accept the original first two diagnoses of ALS. I certainly wasn't going to make that mistake again. It was heart-wrenching at times, but I knew it was my only choice and the one that was disguised with the most love.

Columbia Presbyterian ALS Clinic became our new family of support. We visited once a month with Kevin's doctor, a nurse practitioner, physical, occupational, respiratory, and speech therapists, a registered dietitian, and a social worker. They were wonderful, loving professionals who had the really tough job of meeting the complex medical, psychological, and social needs of ALS patients and their families.

One visit in particular almost brought me to my knees emotionally. Normally, Kevin and I stayed in one exam room, and instead of moving around to each specialist, the specialists took turns visiting us. When the doctor completed his portion of the appointment and prepared to leave the room for the physical therapist to meet with us, he casually mentioned that the tests were in to let us know if Kevin's ALS was familial or sporadic and that he would be back in about 15 minutes to let us know the results. "Familial" ALS means there is more than one occurrence of the disease in a family. "Sporadic" means there is no known history of other family members with the disease and no known cause. The findings of this test were going to reveal to us if the boys had a chance of getting ALS. If Kevin's ALS came back familial, it meant that his children would have a 50% chance of getting it as well.

WHAT????? I knew nothing about this test. Or, quite possibly, it was told to me in a moment when I drifted from my harsh reality and turned off my ability to take one more thing in. The doctor left the room and was quickly replaced by the physical therapist, who began talking as soon as she entered the room. I didn't hear a word she said. My brain was still trying to process the information that I was about to receive from the doctor regarding my kids possibly having ALS when they got older. What the heck was I supposed to do with this information? Did I want to know? Would they want to know? If this was familial, would I share it with them and worry them sick? By this time, I was feeling overwhelmed and frantic. I stopped the meeting. I shared my concerns and uncertainty if knowing the findings of this test was actually what we wanted? This seemed like a big decision to make in 15 minutes, and one that I wanted to choose, not have chosen for me. A family member who was with us told us that she would go find the doctor and tell him that we didn't want to know the results of the test. Fortunately, she privately asked for the results, and when the doctor revealed that they came back "sporadic," she shared the wonderful news with us. Shortly after, the doctor came into the room and confirmed what we had been told; the type of ALS Kevin had was sporadic ALS (the most common form). It affects up to 95% of people with the disease. The results of this test revealed that our children would be spared of this awful disease. Kevin sobbed in relief.

 Such a profound moment of clarity as to the depth and wholeness of a *father's* love even when he is broken.

NINE

NOW

In July 2017, I graduated from iPEC and was officially a certified Life Coach. Kevin cheered me on every step of the way. He was so proud of me and all I was able to accomplish, especially during such a difficult time in our lives. I was proud of myself too.

One story that acted as a beautiful lesson and touched my heart was during an in-person training at iPEC. I was teamed up with a really outgoing, friendly man in my class. During our assignment, tears began to roll down my cheek.. I shared with him that I was trying very hard to be present and focused on what I was learning. I continued by explaining that I had just received a phone call that my father-in-law who I was very close to was not doing well. They informed me that he didn't have much time left. On top of that, I shared that my husband wasn't doing well. It was a lot and I reached a breaking point. He reached his hand over to his wrist and unbuckled his watch and handed it to me. He said I want you to wear this today. I looked at the watch, and it didn't have numbers. It just had the word NOW written across the face. I was so taken back by his kindness and compassion. I wore it all day. When the class was over, I returned the watch and told him how much it meant to me and how it helped me stay present and get through the day. He smiled. The next morning when we got back to class, he called me into the hallway and handed me a gift. It was the NOW watch. He told me that his wife reminded him that when they bought it, it came with two watches. He told me that he never knew why it came with two, and now he does. I was so touched and immediately put on this very meaningful gift from a man who, only a few months prior, was a perfect stranger. At the end of our in-person class time, our instructor asked if anything happened during our training that we would like to share with the class. I told everyone my little story and showed them my new watch. It was definitely a stand-out moment and one that I will always remember with a smile.

 Keep your eyes open, especially when going through difficult times. Glimmers of compassion and human kindness are everywhere.

TEN

LEAD

Now it was time to take these tools and integrate them into our family while navigating the complex art of living life while waiting for death. I was grateful that learning to be a coach taught me so many wonderful skills that would help me be the best leader for my family during such a difficult time in our lives. I certainly didn't know everything, but I was determined to be the best me that I could be for my family.

These were the things that I knew for sure:

- This was the first time that the boys had to deal with anything this difficult and life-changing.
- The boys were going to follow my lead, and I wanted to be mindful and intentional about what that looked like.
- We didn't have a choice about how this would end, but we most definitely had a choice about how it would be until it ended.

- I needed to consider my future self and what she needed, which was peace without regret.
- The boys knew that they would be ok if I was ok, and ok didn't mean hiding my sadness; it meant still being the mom that I had always been – this was an unspoken promise.
- Loving myself was an important part of this journey.

I wrote this love letter to myself before Kevin passed away. I wanted to share in hopes that you will write one to you. You deserve it. You're worth all your love ♥

Here's mine ~

Dear Laurice,

You are the one person I am fully connected with, always. I apologize for times that I've been too hard on you or expected you to be anything but the truest version of yourself. You are truly loved, and I want you to know why. I love you because you are honest, patient, kind, and compassionate. You are a good sister, daughter, wife, mother, aunt, and friend. I love that in the midst of great difficulty, you choose to inspire others rather than fall apart. You are my hero. I admire that you are moving through fear instead of being paralyzed by it. You are strong and take very good care of your family ~ they are counting on you. I love that you genuinely share in other people's happiness, even at a time when your world is filled with so much sadness. I love that you are taking the time to learn more about yourself and trying to grow into the best possible you. But what I love most ~ I love you for loving yourself and understanding the greater importance of self-love and self-care.

Love, Laurice xo

PS: I love that you wrote this and had the courage to share it. You rock!!

So much grieving has already occurred as we are approaching almost two and a half years since this nightmare began. It has certainly been a rollercoaster, and now Kevin was at the point where he couldn't leave our bedroom. Walking was getting more and more difficult and so was keeping on weight. He no longer had the ability to speak, as this monster of a disease had taken that away too. A hospice nurse visited our home twice a week. Kevin became the best air drawer, and I grew into a star guesser. Sometimes the frustration of not being understood would get the best of him which would add a little pressure of guessing well, but we made it work and usually giggled a little. Thinking back, it would have been much easier to have him communicate on an iPad or laptop. I'm not sure why we didn't. Perhaps because we always loved games and loved competing against each other.

By this point, I had made the decision to lead with love, patience, kindness, compassion, understanding, strength, and even laughter when appropriate. Every time I found myself spiraling into a victim mindset, I would quickly ask myself, "Who do you want to be right now?" The answer was very rarely a victim. I would take a breath, a moment, and then recognize where I was headed. I would then choose again. Don't get me wrong, this wasn't perfect, but nothing is – this was me trying to do my best for my husband, my children, myself, and my future self. No one would have blamed me for being a victim, and no judgment for anyone who has or is going through something similar and feels like a victim. I get it.

The boys and I went out for pizza one afternoon. We needed some normal activity away from the reality of so much sadness that permeated the walls of our home. At the beginning of Kevin's illness, while he was still working, I tried very hard each morning to put away anything that had to do with his illness. I didn't want our house to feel like a sick home or a sad one. It was extra work but keeping good energy in the house seemed important for everyone, especially Kevin. By this point, that was no longer possible or helpful. Kevin laid in bed every day with a special power lift recliner in the corner of our room that he would sit in during the day. He also used a bilevel (or BiPAP) breathing machine that delivered pressurized air through a face mask to assist with both inhaling and exhaling, mostly during sleep. As the boys and I sat waiting for our pizza, I thought it would be a good opportunity to share something that had been on my mind. I told them that I recognized that their dad's illness was beyond difficult for them. And how it wasn't fair that, at their young age, they had to watch their father decline. What I wanted them to know was that it was easy to busy themselves with school, sports, and social events. A great way to keep themselves active and not have to face the reality of their father dying. I wanted them to understand that spending quality time with their dad and sharing anything that they wanted him to know would be a gift not only for their dad but also for them – a gift that would last their lifetime. There were no do-overs here, and I wanted to make sure that as they got older, they wouldn't have any regrets. I also wanted to use this time as a check-in and give them the opportunity to share any thoughts, questions or concerns that may feel heavy and on their mind. I believe they appreciated the chat.

It's important to create a safe space for open discussion, active listening and offering a supportive presence for your children. This can be particularly difficult while tending to your own grief. Give yourself grace. (((Hugs)))

ELEVEN

BLESSED

My phone rang, and there was a very kind man on the other end who said hello and introduced himself. He shared that he lived in town and that he knew Kevin. He told me that he had heard about Kevin's illness and that he would like to help our family. He said that every year the Knights of Columbus holds a 5K Turkey Trot event in town, and this year, they would like to sponsor our family. He asked if I would accept. I graciously told him that I would love to accept as long as there wasn't another family that needed it more than ours. He told me that this year they would like to do this for our family and that, in recent years, they have raised up to $7,000. Wow! What a wonderful surprise. A few weeks later, I was driving with my kids through town, and we passed a big sign advertising the Turkey Trot, and it said, "For The Duffy Family." One of my kids yelled, "hey did you see that?" My immediate thought was, "Oh no, what have I done?" For some reason, I thought that this event would happen as it did every year, and the people that like to run these 5K's would participate as they probably did every year. I thought that then they would issue a 5-$7,000 check to our family that we would put towards some of the expenses incurred from Kevin's illness. Boy was I wrong! Before I knew it, family and friends were all talking about it and signing up!! And then I realized that my kids and I needed to be there. "Yikes!" I was gradually becoming more than a little uncomfortable.

The day of the Turkey Trot 5K approached, and the boys and I arrived at the event together. As we pulled into the parking lot, we were quickly met with a sea of cars. "Wow!" someone from the back of the car shouted. "There are a lot of people here." Registration was in the church. We walked in as a group, and the place was packed. There were over 600 people in attendance – beautiful people who wanted to show their love and support to our family. My discomfort rapidly turned into pure gratitude. My heart was exploding with appreciation as my kids got to witness more than 1200 arms wrapping around them, quietly whispering, "we got you." The event was wonderful. We took pictures and videos to bring all the love home to Kevin. What an amazing day. It was probably about a month later that the gentleman running the Turkey Trot called me and came over to meet with us. He was so excited to share that over $51,000 had been raised. He told us that in all the years that they have been hosting this fundraiser, never did they come close to such a collection. My heart was touched in such a way that, to this day, I still find it hard to put it into words. All of the money went into a college fund for the boys. Gratitude is an understatement!

"Blessed are those who give without remembering and always take without forgetting."

~**Elizabeth Bibesco**

TWELVE

STORM

It was the beginning of March 2018. We had a major snowstorm. The streets were almost instantly paved with a thick coat of white powder. The wind was howling, and the snow was accumulating fast. By nighttime, it had gotten so bad that the roads were closed, and a state of emergency was put in place. This was really scary because Kevin was at a point with his illness that he relied on the BiPAP. We needed electricity to operate what has now become a much-needed ventilator. We had a generator but needed gas for it to run if the electricity went out. My brother-in-law lived up the road and somehow made it to our house on foot. The snow was just below his thighs as he trudged down my driveway. I remember my youngest son standing on the roof outside my bedroom window, throwing down an extension cord to my brother-in-law so they could plug in the free-standing generator in the garage. Kevin was so nervous that the electricity was going to go out and we wouldn't have enough gas to run the generator. Every time I walked back into our bedroom, Kevin would air write G-A-S. The outside looked like a real-life snow globe, and Kevin's only wish was uninterrupted power for a machine that helped him breathe. How was this our life? How was this happening to a man that I loved so much? In between my disbelief of what was happening, I would assure him that we wouldn't run out of gas. I couldn't imagine the fear that he must have been feeling. I remember staring out the window, my worry just as heavy as the now two feet of snow that lay before me. "How will we get help if something happens to Kevin during this storm?" Somehow my brother-in-law made it to an open gas station and filled a 5-gallon gas container so we were prepared and could put Kevin's mind to rest. We had gas! Thank God. We had angels that night, for sure!

The next morning, we found a plow to come and clear the driveway. As each scoop of snow got thrown to the side, so did some of the weight that was pressing against my chest. We now had a clear and direct pathway to get Kevin medical help if needed.

The nightmare was over, and I was temporarily relieved before I quickly recognized the importance of deciding if our home was the safest place for Kevin. Apparently, Kevin had the same concern, and together, we made the difficult decision that it was time to go to hospice. I contacted our health care providers from the in-house hospice care Kevin was receiving. They made the arrangements, and within a few days, Kevin was transported to the hospice floor of St. Claire's Hospital in Dover, NJ. We rode together in the transport vehicle as I always wanted him to feel safe. I think holding his hand gave us both some much-needed comfort.

Every day after I got the boys off to school, I would go to St Claire's Hospital and visit Kevin. I would stay there all day and come home in the evening. The older boys now had their driver's licenses, so they would come after baseball practice on days that they weren't buriedwith schoolwork. They would bring Aidan. I was surrounded by family who all lived within a mile from me. This made it convenient for someone to always check on the boys if they were home and I was still at the hospital. We all felt relieved. Kevin felt safe being under 24-hour care, and the boys and I slept better knowing that Kevin was well taken care of during his final weeks of life. Kevin had what they call an End-of-Life Rally. This is when a person facing the end of life "rallies," they become more stable and may even begin eating better. Some describe this phenomenon as a sudden burst of energy before death. Kevin was doing so well that I began questioning our decision for him to be admitted into hospice. It was actually a conversation that I had with the head nurse. This became an especially important conversation after texting Kevin from home, telling him that I was running late. He responded, "No worries, take your time. I ordered a pizza." Have I shared with you that I have a really good sense of humor? I was thinking to myself, *you ordered a pizza?* My next thought - *there has to be a hospice handbook somewhere with very specific rules, and I am certain that "may not order a pizza" is in the top ten.* We definitely weren't your typical hospice family. No one told me I couldn't so one afternoon I crawled into bed with Kevin and we took a nap together. I loved that day. One other time, a group of high school buddies came for a visit. They were telling old stories, laughing and having a great time. Everybody had lots of fun.

It was April 1, 2018, Easter day. My family would all get together and have an amazing Easter dinner. This was how we spent most Sundays. I come from a family of really great cooks (I'm not one of them), and Sunday dinner was special, holiday or not. This Easter Sunday would be different. The kids and I would spend it in the hospice unit of St. Clare's hospital. To our surprise, my amazing sister and brother-in-law met the kids and me at the hospital to visit Kevin. They brought a complete home-cooked dinner for eight with wine and a folding table. We had Easter dinner with Kevin, all together, in his hospital room. I posted a quote that day by Gilda Radner that read,

"I wanted a perfect ending.

Now I've learned the hard way,

That some poems don't rhyme,

And some stories don't

Have a clear Beginning,

Middle, and End.

Life is about not knowing, having to change,

Taking the moment and making the best of it,

Without knowing what's going to happen next."

 And just like the quote read, "life is about taking a moment and making the best of it, without knowing what's going to happen next." I knew we didn't know what would happen next, but we definitely made the best of the moment, and

thanks to my amazing sister and brother-in-law, we nailed it that day. Such a beautiful lesson in honoring, accepting and being fully present in the Now.

THIRTEEN

GOODBYE

Each day was pretty much the same until Friday, April 13th. So predictable, Friday the 13th. You can't make it up! Anyway, I went for a walk with a friend after I got the kids off to school that day. As I have mentioned taking care of myself was an important part of taking care of Kevin and my family. During our walk, I received a phone call from the head nurse at hospice. She told me that I should come to the hospital as Kevin's condition had advanced overnight. I got to the hospital right away. I quickly understood what the nurse meant as I was met with a different stage of Kevin's illness as I walked through his hospital room door.

He didn't seem as alert and appeared weak this particular day. Perhaps this was the beginning of the end. I decided that I would stay overnight with Kevin in his room. The staff brought me something to sleep on and placed it next to Kevin's bed. I stayed there around the clock for the weekend, and on Sunday, it was Kevin's 53rd birthday. Lots of people came to visit that day, and we celebrated his big day. He perked up and seemed like he was back to his old self – at least the old self that checked into hospice weeks prior. We sang Happy Birthday, had cake, and Kevin opened gifts. It was really a nice day of celebrating Kevin. Feeling confident that he had taken a turn for the better, I decided I would sleep at home that night and create some normalcy for the kids. I would be able to get them off to school on Monday morning, and then I would return to the hospital and spend the day with Kevin. I remember walking over to his bed and giving him a kiss. I told him that I was going to go home to be present for the boys and I would be back tomorrow. He looked at me with concern in his expression and slowly shook his head ok. I wasn't convinced that what he was saying and what he was meaning were the same. I said to him, "does ok mean it's important that you are there for the boys and I'm fine? Or does it mean, I know you need to be there for the boys, but I really wish you would stay here with me?" He shook his head yes with a look of need that I had never seen before from him. I walked over to my mom, who hadn't left yet, and said to her, "please round up the troops you need to help you with the boys. I will not be leaving this hospital room until Kevin passes. I will not put him in the position to have to ask me again, not to leave him." She said to me, "don't worry about anything but Kevin." My guess is that he knew, and he was scared. A knowing of his soul that the end was near.

On Tuesday, two days after Kevin's birthday, the nurse had a private meeting with me and said that, in her professional opinion, she believed it was time to increase the prescribed morphine Kevin had been receiving to ensure his comfort and minimize pain as we were at the end. Before dark, Kevin had fallen into a morphine-induced coma. It all seemed to happen so fast. At this point, the boys had all sat with Kevin individually and privately and said their goodbyes. I was certain that he heard every word they spoke. By about 7 pm, it was just Kevin and me. My close friend asked if she could come sit with me. She didn't want me to be alone. I told her that I wasn't certain about a lot at that point but spending the final hours alone with my husband was something that I knew for sure.

I thought a lot about who I needed to be for my children, my husband, myself, and even my future self. I encourage you to think of your future self too. I wanted her to have a life filled with peace and without regret. There were times in the middle of the night when Kevin would wake me and share his high level of anxiety. Rubbing his feet gave him comfort and eased his distress. Although some nights I was beyond exhausted, I knew "she" would want to reflect and know that with patience and kindness, she did everything in her power to make his final months comfortable. I'm so thankful for this gift.

FOURTEEN

GIFT

During Kevin's illness, a dear friend sent out this email and created a special gift for Kevin and our family:

Friends of Kevin Duffy,

I am writing to you in an effort to put together a special gift to share with Kevin Duffy and his family. I coached baseball with Kevin for many years, and like a lot of others, I also coached many Rec games against his teams. I personally have numerous examples of how his influence changed my perspective on leading kids, and I'm betting some of the kids who have been on his teams can also remember an experience or two that really stands out. We know he has had an impact on the lives of many Kinnelon and Butler kids.

What we need:

We would like your help to reach out to as many of the kids Kevin has coached over the years and ask if they would like to write a letter to him sharing how he has impacted them, or share a memory they have of him, or what he has taught them, or maybe even a funny story.

If the kids would like to include a picture of themselves from that team or any pictures they feel are appropriate, that would be great. After receiving these letters/pictures, we will put them together in a book to give to the family. We are not looking to fill a book with generic tributes but would love to capture those little memories of how Kevin may have made an impression.

Also, if any fellow coaches or friends would also like to contribute a story or memory that would be great.

Thank you for your help,

Tom Sienicki

This book was presented to us by our beautiful friends while visiting Kevin in hospice before he began to decline. Kevin was so touched by this thoughtful gift, but he couldn't bring himself to read it. It would create too much emotion for him. He just couldn't do it.

This is one that I would like to share:

Dear Mr. Duffy,

Over my 5 years of baseball and 1 year of football, you were by far one of the best and most important coaches I have ever had. I have had so many life-changing moments with you on and off the field. You have had a positive impact on each and every person that you coached, and that is something that nobody can take away from you. You were always ready to make somebody better no matter what. You could put a smile on my face any day of the week. One important memory I had with you was my first home run. The kid pitching was a good foot taller than me and could throw 70. I was terrified. First pitch I got whizzed right by me. I felt hopeless, and I just wanted to take my 3 strikes and get out of there. But then I looked down the 3rd baseline, and I saw you. And out of everyone who thought I had no chance of even making contact off this kid, you were the only one I could tell believed in me. You didn't even have to say anything; it was just the look you gave me that made me believe in myself. And 3 pitches later, with a 1-2 count, I smacked one over the scoreboard. Hitting the home run was cool and all, but you truly taught me a very important lesson that day. And that lesson was to always believe in yourself no matter what anybody thinks. And no matter how much you are down by or how big the other team is, you always have hope. And in my very next game, I hit 2 more home runs. Without you, I may have never gotten to experience what hitting a home run in little league is like, and I may have quit baseball without you. But if there is one thing that I have learned, it is that with you, there is hope. Thank you for being the best coach I could ever ask for and thank you for making me the person that I am today.

Sincerely, Matt Sienicki

While Kevin lay sleeping on the evening of April 17th and only hours before he was called to heaven, I sat at the edge of his bed as tears rolled down my cheek and read him the entire book. Every letter that was written, he heard. The very impact that he had on so many people while doing the thing that he loved so much – playing and coaching sports. Thank you for giving Kevin the gift of knowing how many hearts he had touched on and off the field.

On April 18th, 2018, at approximately 2 am on the hospice floor of St Claire's hospital, Kevin lost his battle with ALS.

I had the privilege of sitting beside him and gently stroking his face until he took his last breath – my way of letting him know that I was there, not to be afraid and that he was so loved and cherished. Upon my return home, I entered my first son's bedroom and shared the news that dad had passed. He lifted his head from his pillow, nodded, and said, "Mom, are you ok?" I said, "Yes."

There is no easy way to do difficult things. You just do them. With love in your heart and trust in your soul, you just do them.

FIFTEEN

CHOICE

In the early morning of Kevin's death, I spoke to a close friend. I shared with her that although their dad had just passed, I was going to give my boys, all of whom had a baseball game that afternoon, the option to play. Her response, I am certain, was sent through Kevin, "they should play – the game must go on." I sat with each child individually that morning and reminded them that they had a game that afternoon. I explained to them that playing in it was their decision and that there was no right or wrong, good or bad, in their answer. This was a decision that was about them and only them. It shouldn't be made based on what any of the other boys were going to do. Two were immediate yeses, and the other two were hesitant. One of them shared that he thought maybe it was weird to play ball on the day that their dad died. I said, "well, it depends on how you look at it. Playing baseball was something that you and your brothers did the most with your dad. What better way to honor him than play on the day of his death? And today, he'll have the best seat in the house." And, of course, I reminded him never to make decisions based on what other people might think and to always follow his own heart. Glennon Doyle says, "Every life is an unprecedented experiment. This life is mine alone. So I have stopped asking people for directions to places they've never been. There is no map. We are all pioneers." I didn't want any of my kids to ask anyone for directions to places that they had never been. Not even me. I was there to support, not choose. This was an important time for each of us to practice honoring our own personal truth with certainty, conviction, and maybe even confusion at times. I knew we would all have different needs and speaking up about them unapologetically was mandatory in my opinion. We all needed to take care of ourselves and each other, and that's exactly what we did as we moved along on our individual and collective grief journey. This wasn't only the loss of a parent but also the loss of love, guidance, security and support for the boys. I knew it would look different for each of them – not easy to manage while going through my own grief, but nothing about any of this was easy.

All four boys decided to play baseball that sunny afternoon. What an amazing day. My youngest son was playing at the same school next to the field the older boys were playing on. The older boys were playing Kevin's high school alma mater, and before the game, the athletic director had a moment of silence in Kevin's memory and shared a few thoughtful words. I was surrounded by friends and kids, all of whom knew Kevin and loved our family. We won the game! The boys were so happy that they all decided to play, and we all knew Kevin watched with pride. Watching our boys play ball was one of Kevin's favorite things to do. How beautiful that he got to do it with all the angels on the day he arrived in heaven.

Sometimes the choices that may appear to be different turn out to be the most beautiful. Follow your heart and you will never be lost.

SIXTEEN

WARRIOR

Planning a wake and funeral can feel overwhelming in the face of loss and grief. Thankfully I didn't have to do it alone. Family and friends all joined together, making this process manageable and flow with ease. Everyone took on a role. It felt seamless. It was their way of taking care of me and something that they could physically do to help with a situation that often left them feeling helpless. I was so grateful. I had a much-needed team.

The sendoff was really important to me. I wanted it to be beautiful and honor Kevin in every way. I always knew that I would give the eulogy. I had prepared it with some of my high school besties a few weeks before Kevin's passing. It was edited by my sister-in-law and tweaked by me until it was perfect. Picture boards were made and displayed, highlighting the beautiful life Kevin lived. A video thoughtfully put together by a member of the "team," was playing to carefully chosen music on a large TV in the church foyer as friends and family entered the service.

Kevin's request was to be cremated. On the coffin, we placed a large photo of him. The picture we chose was so vibrant. He was wearing a lilac-colored button-down shirt, and he had the warmest, most contagious smile. This picture beautifully highlighted his handsome features – his piercing icy-blue eyes and strong cheekbones. It was a picture of Kevin that we all knew before this awful disease stole his spark and vitality.

I purposely did not wear black to the services. I chose navy pants, a white blouse with navy trim for the wake, and a medium-toned blue dress with blush-colored shoes for the funeral. Yes, I lost my husband, but I wasn't willing to lose myself and identify with a label that was given to me without my consent. I don't even like the word widow. I certainly wasn't going to dress like one. Who makes these rules anyway? And why are people following them? And why we're on the subject, let's change the word widow to warri♥r. Yeah, that feels so much better. Widow feels so powerless. We are warriors working through feeling the pain of losing our partners and taking on the sorrow of our children losing their dad. We have no shield. We know the only way out is through, and the only way to heal is to feel. This is painful stuff, and there is nowhere to hide. Yeah, wow, we are total warriors!

The wake was from 2-4 pm and then 6-8 pm. We had a break in between the two time slots where we went back to my house, and food was delivered for everyone to eat. Only immediate family joined. I spent the time in my bedroom alone. I needed time away from all the noise to process everything that was happening. While everyone was refueling physically, I needed to refuel mentally and emotionally. I knew it was very important for me to take care of my children's mother. I also knew that part of taking care of myself meant a willingness to receive help ~ fortunately, many were offering, and I was graciously accepting.

Rather than handing out memorial cards at Kevin's wake and funeral, we did something different. Something we knew Kevin would love. In honor of my husband, a man whose heart was always filled with love and compassion, we had kindness cards made and gave them out at the wake and funeral services. The hope was to generate goodness with random acts of kindness. I truly believe that the benefits of kindness can be contagious and have a ripple effect that spreads outwards.

This is how it works: do something kind (pre-pay for someone's coffee, bring a meal to a neighbor, buy an ice cream from the ice cream truck for other kids, leave money for a snack on the vending machine, drop off a bottle of wine to a friend having a bad day, etc.), attach the kindness card to your deed. The receiver will then pass that card along attached to their own act of kindness. My hope was to shower this world with a touch of kindness in honor of my husband, Kevin Duffy, one of the kindest men I knew.

We gave out over 2000 cards, and about ten months after Kevin's services, I actually received one back at a local coffee shop. That was a great day! Some of the special acts of kindness that stand out and have been shared with me are:

The owner of a nail salon gave a kindness card with a free service to a client who was fighting cancer.

On the one-year anniversary of Kevin's death, a teacher brought bagels, juice, and coffee for the faculty and left kindness cards for everyone to take.

I shared one at a local drive-thru coffee shop and asked to pay for the person behind me. For some reason, the barista had gotten unusually backed up, and my order was taking a long time – I was able to see the person I was extending my kindness to from my rearview mirror. She was getting very agitated at the wait. Kindness was exactly what she needed, and I'm sure it changed her day. So much power in kindness!

One woman bought a birthday cake at a bakery to be given to the next person ordering one and asked the person helping her to please attach the kindness card to it. Honoring someone who passed by paying for a cake to celebrate someone's life. Wow!!

It's been over 4 years since we handed out the kindness cards, and someone shared with me that they recently received one at a local coffee shop. And the ripple continues...

In lieu of flowers for Kevin's funeral, we asked that people consider making a donation that would be put towards Kinnelon High School athletics in some way. We had some ideas but weren't committed to any one thing. One of Kevin's favorite places was that football field – what better way to honor him than to use the money for some sort of an athletic improvement at the High School which his kids would all be attending? We had a bit over $5000. I knew we would come up with something amazing, but never did I think it would be this amazing!

I received a call from the KHS Athletic Director that a large colt statue became available to purchase (our school mascot is a colt) for almost the exact amount that was donated. Not a coincidence. A blessing. He suggested using the money for the statue and placing it in front of the school campus with a remembrance plaque for Kevin. I loved, loved, loved the idea. I designed the plaque and used the same theme from the eulogy, "the game must go on." It reads,

A dedication to

Kevin Duffy

For his passion and commitment to

Kinnelon Athletics

The game must go on...

Forever in our hearts ~

Coach Duffy

It turned out amazing as it sits on a stone platform with the plaque built in and a spotlight that shines brightly, revealing all its beauty.

The administration planned an unveiling of the statue ceremony. It was scheduled during halftime at one of our football games. Those organizing announced that this particular game would be a "red out" in recognition of ALS. Our more than talented and beautiful cheerleaders wore red socks and painted red lines under their eyes. Some wore red beads around their neck. The students and families who attended all wore red. Red streamers decorated the metal bleachers. It was amazing! This game was also an ALS fundraiser. 50/50 tickets were sold, and a woman from the opposing team won. She donated her winnings back to join our collection to help strike out this dreaded disease. Her own father died of ALS. Just take a second and think about this ~ Annually, ALS is responsible for two deaths per 100,000 people ~ what are the chances that the winner of the 50/50 at a small-town football game also lost a loved one as a result of this awful illness? We hugged. It was a special moment.

A new tradition was created at the high school. Our athletes now touch the colt statue before each home game. Wow! My kids have been given a daily reminder of how many lives their amazing father has touched ~ a priceless gift. And this all happened during the only year that all four boys would be in the same school together, and it was the high school where they would see the statue every morning as they walked toward the school's entrance.

Thank you again to everyone who helped make this happen, those who attended, and to so many who have taken their arms and wrapped them around the boys and me with countless acts of kindness, many prayers, and an abundance of love. We will forever be grateful.

After about two weeks following Kevin's passing and taking some time to just be, I felt ready to share on social media. This is what I wrote:

For those of you who may not know, my beautiful and courageous husband lost his battle with ALS on April 18th. Although still consumed with sadness, I feel relieved that he has now been given back all that had been so cruelly taken away. I miss my best friend and the most amazing father to our four boys, yet I am truly grateful for the time we had together and the immense love we shared. Some days are hard, and I feel lost and heartbroken. Some days I'm ok. Sometimes I cry. Sometimes I laugh. Grief is not linear. There are no rules ~ no timetables. In the days ahead, I will follow the lead of my emotions with no expectation of what the day, hour, or moment will bring. I will feel it fully, knowing this is the only path to the other side of pain. Some days I feel a surge of strength. Some days I don't feel strong at all. I am, however, committed to staying open to the beauty and love that surrounds me, staying true to myself, and remaining hopeful in the midst of this uncertain storm of emotions. One thing I know for sure is that there is a message in every tragedy. I will firmly hang on to the lessons, as I have already learned that death has a way of teaching us so much about life.

The experience may break your soul into a thousand little pieces. And like a beautiful mosaic, each fragile piece will meticulously be placed back together differently and brilliantly. Be open to the colorful transformation.

You have the power to say, "This is not how my story will end"

SEVENTEEN

HEAL

It was like a hurricane had blown through, and we all held on for dear life. Never really sure how we would get through, but always knowing that getting through was our only choice. Filled with anxiety and no defense, we were forced to just wait. As uncertain and scared as we sometimes felt, we also knew the direct impact of the storm hadn't yet occurred. And then that dreadful and much anticipated day came and went. And you think the storm is over when actually it's just a different storm you find yourself in. I stood in stillness, overwhelmed by all that had occurred. And now, before me, is the aftermath and the enormous job of picking up all the pieces. And while your heart is aching for what has been lost, you are desperate to make sure that all the pieces get put back together in such a way that your four beautiful children, who are so deeply relying on you, have faith that it really is going to be ok.

It was a summer filled with patience, sadness, kindness, emptiness, stillness, understanding, strength, uncertainty, love, fear, grace, and compassion. So many different emotions. So many different feelings. And my commitment to be with each and every one of those feelings that showed up on any given day.

I sought therapy and grief counseling for the five of us as a family during Kevin's illness and after his death. I hired a coach for myself 6 months after Kevin passed away. This provided me a safe place to unload, untangle, and sometimes even understand what exactly I was feeling. A place to explore the many complicated thoughts and feelings that accompany loss. We talked at length about not rushing through the grief process and how to model healthy grieving for my boys. We focused on my strong desire to be present and true to myself. Also, how sharing my grief would give the kids permission to work through their grief individually and in their own way.

Of course, I was also surrounded by wonderful family and friends that were significant in my healing process. One thing that I knew for sure was that this was my grief journey and unique to me and that because Kevin had a terminal illness, my grieving process started long before he died.

September rolled around rather quickly, and so did the new school year. The older boys were seniors in high school, and my youngest was an incoming freshman. I loved that they were all under one roof and together in the same school. The only year in the twelve years of their education, this would occur, and the timing could not have been better. It gave me comfort. I hoped that it gave them comfort too. They had a lot of love and support from the staff and administration at their high school. Many eyes watched out for them and paid attention to the needs of four boys who had lost a little piece of their hearts and rock-solid stability. I was given a whole lot of peace, placing them in the hands of so many amazing people.

And life continued. The boys had active social lives and played dual sports. I attended all their games which was always one of my favorite things to do. Friends and family remained very supportive and showed our family a lot of continued love and kindness. Every once in a while, we would run into a glitch, like the first time two of the boys had to dress up for school because they had a basketball game, and a dress shirt and tie were mandatory. They ran into my room for help. It was at that moment we all realized no one but dad knew how to correctly tie a tie. Oops! Fortunately, they were all pretty laid back and draped the tie around their neck and scurried off to school without worry. They asked a male teacher to help them. Finally, one of the boys YouTubed it, and he now successfully ties a tie with ease. Good ole YouTube!

 Allow sadness

Sit with it

Listen to what it needs you to hear

Notice where you feel it in your body

Be with it until you decide that you've spent enough time together

When you feel ready, say thank you for sharing and show sadness to the door

Find joy

Repeat...

It's in the process of allowance rather than resistance that we heal.

EIGHTEEN

RISE

As you can imagine being a teenage boy dealing with the unwanted emotions of grief and having a mom as a life coach is always a great time. I love to share, talk about feelings, and create depth and meaning in our conversations, and they… Well, they would pretty much rather do anything else! While I've learned to meet each of them where they are rather than where I want them to be, they have gotten comfortable opening up and becoming more emotionally expressive rather than suppressive. Although to this day, they sometimes hit me with, "Mom, it's not that deep," and I respect that cue. We have all done a pretty good job finding a healthy balance, and I think that we're all better for it.

At this point on our shared grief journey, my approach to recovery was a little different than that of my kids. Whereas they were more focused on their social lives, I was less preoccupied with social activity, although still getting out with close friends and family. While the boys were seeking a normal daily routine with things familiar to them, I was committed to increasing my threshold for being uncomfortable. I knew stepping out of my comfort zone was an issue when Kevin was healthy, but somehow, it was easy to overlook in the busyness of a large family. For example, if I was nervous about driving somewhere I had never been, Kevin would take me. This was no longer the case when Kevin's illness progressed and certainly shined a light on my fear of the unknown. I knew I had to address my fear and discomfort. I began to chip away at what sometimes felt like a brick wall that blocked me from the opportunity to do what I wanted. This felt like the roadmap to freedom and independence. After all, my clearly defined life that felt so safe was now upside down. Why not take it a step further and forge forward into the unknown? So, this is what I did. I asked friends to invite me to do things that scared me. Sounds awful, right? I know. I thought the same thing but knew I had to go all in with this new life that was forced upon me. What I soon realized was that it wasn't actually in doing the scary thing that caused me to feel intimidated and overwhelmed – it was the *anticipation* of doing it that I most struggled with. The actual doing wasn't the problem. It was the thinking about the doing that made my palms sweaty and my heart race. I now understood where the work was. What you must know is that the benefits were amazing and outweighed every bit of the anticipatory anxiety.

Here are a few of my stepping stones out of the comfort trap:

I drove into New York City and walked across the Brooklyn Bridge with a girlfriend. It was the driving part in and out of Manhattan that caused me discomfort, and I did it! As I left the city feeling empowered, I looked up and, to my amazement, saw painted graffiti on the side of a building that read FEARLESS ~ a sign placed perfectly for me to see. I knew it wasn't a coincidence and would become the title of my new story.

I drove my family and a girlfriend to Yankee Stadium in the Bronx, NY. A definite challenge and success.

I picked up my girlfriend from Newark Airport. This was one of the few uncomfortable adventures that I needed to do by myself. Halfway anyway.

I visited California with a friend, where she had me meet her at the airport and navigate our way to the correct gate. We attended a three-day Influencer event by a brilliant thought leader, Brendon Burchard. So many amazing speakers! So much growth!

I visited Portugal for 8 days and lived with a large group of people, some of whom I was meeting for the first time. So many opportunities to be in new situations and experience the unfamiliar.

I traveled alone to Oregon for a retreat with my mastermind program, meeting my business coach and fellow coaches in person for the first time. I knew the growth that would occur in traveling solo and navigating a new state across the country would be just as expansive as what I learned at the retreat. Both experiences were fantastic!

I visited Paris as a single person with three married couples. I was committed to acting as the gentle observer on this trip. Noticing how it felt for me as a single woman to be traveling with only married couples. It occurred to me that it may make me feel sad, and I may want to go home. I made a choice before I left not to make my feelings good or bad. I decided to instead use them as information to guide me more thoroughly on this journey of connection, understanding, and development I was having with myself.

My beautiful relationship with me. I had an amazing trip and never once wanted to go home.

I knew that stepping outside my comfort zone would provide me with big rewards, such as more freedom, independence, and growth. My business coach challenged me to begin getting uncomfortable being comfortable. Yikes! I get it, though. Leaving your comfort zone certainly leads you to quite a growth zone. I can't say I'm at that point of being uncomfortable feeling comfortable, but it's always good to have future goals.

This is how I managed the anxious anticipation of continuing on this journey of growth.

I arrived home from Portugal and, that same night, visited friends and family. I felt amazing. I made the conscious decision to really take in how great I felt. To absorb the feeling of satisfaction and pride in having done the scary thing gave me. I actually paused and thought about how the evening, and probably the whole week, was going to be so much better because of my leap into the unfamiliar. I honored myself for this wonderful feeling of accomplishment and for stretching myself beyond what felt comfortable. I marinated in that feeling. I locked it in. I can now call in that feeling anytime I choose. Now every time I have to do something that puts me in a place of discomfort that I know will spark personal growth and the voice gets loud, I simply shift into the feeling I had on the evening I arrived home from Portugal. It's bigger than the voice. It wins every time.

 The acronym F.E.A.R. stands for

"Face. Everything. And. Rise." Remember that.

NINETEEN

PRESENT

Our first Christmas after losing Kevin was approaching. I knew that waking up and surrounding the Christmas tree to open gifts without Kevin was going to be too much to bear. I decided we needed a new morning tradition. And a puppy! My girlfriend drove the 5-hour round trip with me to pick up an 8-week-old golden retriever. It was a Christmas morning surprise for the boys, so we dropped the puppy off at my sister's house, where he would stay hidden from my kids until Christmas. The new tradition was to wake up on Christmas morning, open gifts, and have breakfast with my parents, sister, brother-in-law, and niece's family. We all lived within a mile of each other, so this was very convenient. We all walked into my sister's house. I was first. It was straight out of a Hallmark movie. The puppy was in a basket, under the tree, with a bow. The boys walked in behind me, still half asleep, and while I was so excited about the big surprise, they were....well.... underwhelmed. They really weren't terribly excited. Who doesn't get so excited about a puppy in a basket under the Christmas tree?? I'll chalk it up to them still being half asleep. My niece has little ones, so it was pretty early - especially early for teenage boys. As the morning continued and they became more awake, they were loving the little guy. We named him Fenway because the boys (and Kevin) are big Red Sox fans. Fenway has brought more love into our home and has been the greatest addition to our family.

Before I knew it, summer was approaching, and the older boys had graduated from high school. Time was flying, and the thought of three goodbyes in my near future as I would be sending them off to college was a bit heart-wrenching. As a graduation gift, I took them and my youngest son to an all-inclusive resort in Mexico. My sister and her whole family came too. It was a wonderful vacation. We had a lot of fun. It was on that trip that I was once again reminded of the importance of being in the present and in the now. I wrote a blog while sitting in a little coffee shop on our trip that also acts as a valuable lesson.

 As a gift to my sons for their high school graduation, we took a vacation with our extended family to an all-inclusive resort in Mexico. As a recent widow with three soon-to-be college freshmen, and another one in high school, I knew that the trip was a bit of a stretch financially. But, in choosing to take some time out for my family, I made lasting memories with my sons and learned a great lesson along the way. Sometimes it is in giving that we, ourselves, receive the biggest gift.

In a world filled with schedules and to-do lists (and with four children there are a lot of those!), I've come to realize that vacations are not a luxury but a necessity. There aren't any distractions or responsibilities when on vacation. Vacations aren't about where you are; they're about where you aren't. Being at home means responsibilities and routine.

Sometimes we get lost in the patterns of the mundane duties that our daily lives demand, making it difficult to live in the moment because we are always trying to stay ahead of everything we NEED to do and ignoring what we WANT to do. We are constantly on autopilot, and we don't even realize it.

Vacation helps to break the cycle of living in that semi-unconscious state.

Vacations make it possible to recharge our minds, bodies, and souls and present us with unlimited opportunities to learn and breathe new life into our routines. It's a process of discovery. Vacation makes it possible for us to dwell in the now just a little bit longer. When we have no worries, no fears, and no pressing concerns, it's a lot easier to live in the present and live for the moment.

Being present is about slowing things down enough to feel and experience what is happening in the moment, not what happened in the past and not what will happen in the future. Vacation has a way of pulling us out of the busy and guiding us into the present.

Through my journey to becoming a life coach and losing my husband, the lens through which I see the world has changed. I now appreciate that there isn't always time to wait. Life is happening now.

Some of us keep waiting for the right time to live the life we desire. We want to work more, save more, and wait for the mortgage to be paid off and the kids to graduate from college. The list goes on and on but guess what? There will always be something else. We always think that tomorrow is better than today. Today is the tomorrow you planned for yesterday. *The only time is NOW. Take that vacation and enjoy the moment. Emily Dickinson says it best, "forever is composed of nows."*

I know this to be true because I have lived a life where I was constantly focused on all the wonderful things that were going to happen in the future, a month or a year from now. I was always living in the "soon," never in the "now." I used to live in a world where the future held success and happiness, and the present was never enough. I was always trying to get to the destination, never realizing the journey was actually the destination.

The precious gift that I took home from my vacation was learning how to slow down and stay happy in the moment. The best part is that you can practice slowing down and enjoying the present moment anywhere. Where you are doesn't matter. What does matter is that you stop for a few weeks, a few days, or even a few hours and recharge. Take time to pause life and get aligned with who you are and what is most important. Shift out of autopilot and realign with your deeper desires.

You will be amazed at what you find not only in the outside world but, even more so, within yourself.

TWENTY

CHANGES

It wasn't too long after Kevin's death that we were hit with the devastation of the COVID-19 pandemic. All of us being home at the same time didn't happen that often. It definitely shined a light on Kevin's absence. We were also soon approaching what would have been our 25th wedding anniversary (see the blog at the end of the chapter). Between that and the inability to be busy, I had some difficult days. I missed having another adult in the house. My other half. My partner. Someone I could hand the baton off to when I didn't have the answer, the energy, the patience... or all of the above. The truth is, I missed my husband and my children's dad. On the flip side, I learned a lot during the lockdown. Here are my takeaways:

My Top 20 Lessons of 2020

1. Never again take small things for granted – practice gratitude each and every day.
2. Do the right thing even when others are not. Integrity is a gift we give ourselves.
3. Find ways to serve.
4. Look outside the box. Opportunities are everywhere.
5. Say thank you more.
6. It shouldn't take a pandemic to slow us down – slow down.
7. Make time for loved ones. Nothing is guaranteed.
8. No matter what happens in life, we always get to choose our attitude toward it.
9. Flexibility is a super power.
10. Positive thinking goes a longer distance when followed by positive action.
11. Learning technology IS possible.
12. Go inward. Feelings are data.
13. Spending time alone has reminded us of the importance of liking who we are.
14. We are all connected.
15. Doing your best and giving it your best means different things on different days.
16. When we attempt to control our world, we allow our world to control us.
17. None of us is stronger than all of us.
18. We haven't all been equally affected by the challenges of this year – less judgment, more compassion.
19. Where there is a struggle, there is an opportunity to grow.
20. Always say I Love you.

It was May 2021. We were now easing back into life after 2 years of the pandemic. My elderly parents, who live only a mile away, have survived the pandemic without getting sick. Thankful is an understatement. My mom was 83, and my dad was 88 at this point. They had just celebrated their 63rd wedding anniversary. My dad would always tease and say, "you get less time for murder!" My good sense of humor was definitely passed down from my parents. They had a great love for laughter. They were also beautiful examples of love and commitment. Their family was their number one priority. I have two brothers, a sister, and many nieces and nephews. Sunday dinners were a weekly occurrence.

In September of 2021, both my parents were fully vaccinated, and we were all lulled into a false sense of security. My mom shared the news that both she and my dad weren't feeling well and tested positive for Covid-19. I lost my breath for a second but then quickly remembered that they were both vaccinated and felt confident that they would both recover. We felt helpless but hopeful that everything would be ok and life as we knew it would continue.

After a few days, my mom seemed to be getting worse. Each day she would tell us that she thought she was getting a little better. That wasn't the case. My sister called her doctor and shared our mom's condition. He recommended that she go to a hospital for monoclonal antibody treatment. My brother took her. That afternoon, both of our parents were admitted to the hospital. Our father was able to recover, and unfortunately, due to complications, my mother was not. As for many, devastation struck as well as disbelief. Our hearts were broken.

The day of my mother's funeral was also senior night for Aidan's high school football team. This is a night to celebrate each senior players' final year playing high school football. We left the cemetery, ate an early dinner with family, and headed right over to the field. The five of us had to smile for pictures. Manage the sadness of losing my mom and their nana while wanting to be in the spirit of celebration for Aidan on an important night. We pulled from the strength we were given when Kevin left us and went to heaven. We learned that we had a reserve to tap into when needed. We knew where to find it. We knew we had each other. And then something amazing happened. My dad, my children's pop-pop, walked down the field with us. Two of the older boys stood on each side of him, arm in arm, and helped him make it down the field as we were all announced. Pop-pop was so honored and delighted to be part of this special night. He was one of the boys' biggest fans and attended almost all their games.

Weeks passed after losing our mom. It soon became obvious that living alone wasn't a good option for my dad. He needed more care and attention at the age of 88 and after dealing with such a big loss. Sixty-three years of his life were spent with my mom. He didn't know life without her. His grief, at times, was harder for me to endure than my own.

Two months later, we made the decision for my dad to move in with me. I had a basement with a bedroom and bathroom that we were able to turn into a cute apartment. I knew that he would feel comfortable with us and enjoy the busyness of our home. He always wanted a dog, and now he had Fenway.

One night at dinner, my dad shook his head in disbelief and shared that he missed my mom so much and that life can be so cruel.

My response ~ *it depends on how you look at it. You had a beautiful marriage with a woman you loved very much and who loved you back just as much. What a privilege and a fulfilling life. Thank you for the gift. Because of you, I got to be part of such a wonderful love story. I'll always be so grateful.*

The conversation continued. *I shared that this was just a pause. One day you and mom will be together again. For now, let's explore your purpose. Why mom and not you?* He nodded his head. "I have no idea." *I shared perhaps it's to be a male figure for the boys. Maybe, just maybe, you are still here because the boys and I need you.* He smiled big— the power of purpose.

Twenty-five years ago today, I vowed to take you, Kevin, to be my husband, to have and to hold you from that day forward, for better, for worse, for richer, for poorer, in sickness and in health, to love and to cherish, 'til death do us part, according to God's holy law, in the presence of God.

On this day, twenty-five years ago, never did I think, 'til death do us part would come sooner rather than later. Never did I think that in sickness and in health meant three years of so much suffering. Never did I think to have and to hold would be clenching your hand and stroking your face until you took your last breath.

Today, twenty-five years after one of the happiest days of my life, two and a half years after the day you left us, never did I think you would leave me with so much love that I would be able to share it and spread it onto so many that cross my path. Never did I think you would leave me with so much strength that I would be able to carry our family with so much certainty and grace. Never did I think that you would leave our boys filled with so much of your kindness, determination, love, and joy that pride would become an understatement. Never did I think that you would leave the five of us filled with so much gratitude for knowing, learning, and loving you rather than bitterness for losing you.

Happy 25th anniversary to the love of my life. You will continue and always be the light that keeps me shining!

TWENTY-ONE

MISSION

Twenty-one was Kevin's football number. He loved that number. In 2021, I started something that I'm very proud of and felt really good about.

The older boys were graduating high school, and I attended their Senior awards ceremony in June 2020. Students were given well-deserved scholarships for respected categories such as beautifully written essays, academic achievements, and excellence in athletics, and the list went on and on. While these were all amazing areas that should absolutely be recognized, I realized that there wasn't a scholarship for kindness. In a world where there is so much focus on bullying, there is not enough recognition for all the kindness that our students are demonstrating. Kindness matters too.

In the winter of 2020, I called our local high school guidance department and told them I wanted to start a

Kindness Matters Scholarship for the graduating senior class. Yup! The class of 2021. Just worked out that way? Nah... I don't believe in coincidences.

The process is as follows:

All teachers in each school are asked to nominate a Senior student for the award. This person doesn't need to be one of their current students, but it must be someone whose behavior and character have been observed to exemplify kindness. Each teacher provides a short explanation as to why they chose this student. Guidance collects the nominations and reviews and chooses the recipient.

We gave the scholarship to two students at our local high school the first year we offered it, and my company, A Mindful Journey, funded it. The second year I created it as a nonprofit organization, Kindness Matters Mission. We collected donations from beautiful people that I feel so much gratitude towards. As a result of their kindness and generosity, we were able to give the scholarship to three high schools. One of them being Kevin's high school alma mater. The power of turning pain into purpose. Wow!

This is the speech that I give at the award ceremony:

Good evening. My name is Laurice Duffy. I am a Life Coach and the founder of A Mindful Journey. After attending other award ceremonies and seeing so many amazing awards being given out for beautifully written essays, high academic achievements, and athletic talent, I thought it was important that we send the message to our youth that kindness matters too. Kindness has been a theme and a way of honoring my late husband, Kevin Duffy, who died far too young from ALS four years ago. He was a man whose heart was always filled with love and compassion. The impact he had on people, and particularly the youth, as both dad and coach, will always be remembered. In this spirit, A Mindful Journey has started a non-profit foundation, "The Kindness Matters Mission." Inspired by Kevin, this scholarship is being awarded to a student who is an example of kindness.

Congratulations to (name of student), this year's recipient of the Kindness Matters Scholarship.

I am so proud of this scholarship and how it allows me to bring Kevin's memory along with me on a mission to plant seeds of kindness one high school at a time.

 Finding a way to honor a loved one who has passed helps us to celebrate their life and ease the agony of their death.

TWENTY-TWO

HOPE

The holidays quickly approached. We were getting together with a large group on Christmas day (2021), so I had the boys get tested for COVID the day before. No one was sick, and it was actually just to be responsible and give everyone peace of mind. To my surprise, two of the boys came home with a positive test. My first thought was, "Thank goodness they got tested," and then my second thought hit me like a punch in the stomach! No Christmas with our extended family. Our first Christmas without our mom, and I won't see my siblings? My poor dad! Two kids were stuck in their rooms for all of Christmas Eve and Christmas day. This will be horrible!

And then I noticed the rabbit hole I was going down. I paused and took a breath. I wanted to choose differently. I reminded myself that this is out of our control and will be what we make it be. Just like every other circumstance in life, we get to choose. It was a quiet two days filled with ease, comfort, and peace. There was nowhere to go, no place to be, no need to get ready, and nothing to prepare. It was just what I needed. I even had time to write a poem that acted as a much-needed lesson.

 ### *Covid Christmas Poem*

Twas' the night before Christmas
And all through the day
The kids were out testing
To make sure they're ok

If even one tested positive
we were out as a group
No Christmas dinner
Maybe take out or soup

I got the phone call
Mom, my test is a yes
I'm stuck in quarantine
'til Monday at best!

It was then that I realized
Christmas was done
no one would have us
no one would come

Raising Hope

So I sent a group text
and shared the bad news
let's do our best
To create a win, not a lose

I read, and I rested
Dinner was brought
making the best of a situation
my children were taught

Many thanks to the universe
You always seem to know
when it's time to hit stop
Even if my mind says go

What at first appeared awful
was soon found to be
a blessing in disguise
As quiet was key

Stop and pay attention
no need to fret
when you truly surrender
what you need, you will get

It was a different Christmas and one that we will definitely never forget. As you can imagine, with triplets and another child two and a half year's younger, we had a lot of wild, busy, and fun Christmas mornings. Choosing to find the things that were right about this particular year instead of what was wrong with it, made all the difference for us.

Summer came and went faster than most summers I can remember. The boys are now amazing young adults. I often think about the unique friendship that Kevin would have had with each of them. The grown-up father-son bond that so many are fortunate enough to have in their life. With effort, I shift my thinking back to what all the boys have gained by having Kevin as their dad rather than all they have lost due to his passing. It takes practice. I work on it almost every day. I think I did a pretty good job overall. I'm confident Kevin is proud of each and every one of us. I'm proud of all of us too.

As I'm writing the final pages of this book, all four boys are preparing to leave for college. I will officially become an empty nester in two short weeks. I find myself asking the same question on repeat, "how did we get here?" It's in the feelings attached to that question that I'm reminded – grief does not discriminate and is not only associated with death but also with endings, including kids leaving home.

What I now know for sure is that it's what we choose to do with endings that matters most. Hope provides a way forward and lives in each and every one of those choices.

What will you choose?

LESSONS

I truly believe that our pain is here to teach us rather than to punish us. I think that when we can wipe away the tears, get past the anger, and see with clarity, a message is usually awaiting us. Something to learn. A takeaway is necessary for our growth. These events in our life serve a higher purpose. Wayne Dyer says, "Change the way you look at things, and the things you look at change." Maybe we need to look at it differently. What if these lessons are what expand our soul and the reason for us having this complex and sometimes confusing human experience. *To learn, grow, and evolve.* Here are some of the valuable lessons that I learned on my grief journey:

Lesson: ♥ **Life is about our ability to adjust and accept what is. It's about how we embrace plan B.**

Plan A is always our first choice ~ the plan where everything works out perfectly and exactly the way we want it to. You know, the ideal plan with the happily-ever-after ending. Well, I learned that sometimes plan A and what actually happens are two very different things. This is where the choice becomes ours ~ wallow in self-pity or shift gears, roll up our sleeves, and design a new plan? Of course, we can wallow for a while, but we can't live there. Life is often an exercise in the art of flexibility. It's not meant to be perfect and, at times, may feel less than fair. Be willing to be willing and when you're ready, embrace plan B.

Lesson: **Be kind. You have absolutely no idea what people are dealing with in their life.**

I entered the store after dropping off my children's clothes to the dry cleaners for their dad's funeral services. I lost my husband, and my children lost their dad only two short days prior. I was dressed, and my hair was surprisingly brushed. I realized that I looked like every other person in that store. Nothing separated me from the people who were shopping for a fun dinner party or buying drinks for their kid's baseball team. No one knew that I was grieving the death of my husband. We all looked the same.

Lesson: **Never underestimate the profound power of touch ~ a hug, a hand squeeze, or a rub on the back — it's a powerful, nonverbal language that helps us connect, heal, and soothe. When you're feeling helpless with those who are sick or filled with sadness, simply hold their hand and allow the limitless effects of love to soar.**

I went to my son's baseball game one afternoon. It was a very difficult day. It was important that I was present and there for the boys. I entered the stadium and sat down next to a friend whose son also played on the team. I couldn't control the tears. I tried. Sometimes we get so caught up in protecting those around us from the discomfort of our emotions that we forget to take care of ourselves. It didn't matter. On this day, I didn't have the strength. Clearly, there were no words to comfort me or to change the reality of my situation. She didn't say a word. She gave me a chance to sit down and stay with my feelings. Then in the silence of so much grief, she simply reached her hand over to mine and held it. This said so much more to me than any words could have. I felt loved, supported, and connected.

Lesson: **Hearing stories about loved ones that have passed are a beautiful reminder of the impact they had while they were here. Never a reminder that they're gone. There is so much healing in remembering.**

Never be afraid to bring up someone's loved one that passed away. Risk discomfort. Know with confidence that you are not reopening an old wound. I light up when people share a memory of Kevin with me. It's a gift. It makes me smile.

Lesson: **Sharing our sadness and allowing uncomfortable feelings to move through us is an act of courage, truth, and self-love. There is so much beautiful that lives on the other side of suffering in silence.**

Friends and family created a safe space for me to honor and express my feelings. Sometimes that meant sitting in it with me, and sometimes it meant sharing my unexpected flood of emotion and excusing myself from a social event to give myself whatever I needed at that moment.

Lesson: **It's not in loss and sadness that we lose our way; it's in forgetting where to find comfort.**

I arrived at a barbecue one Sunday afternoon on my sister's back deck. A few people began to talk about different projects they were going to be doing around their homes. It struck me. Very unexpectedly. I didn't have my partner to make these desire lists with. I struggled to hold back my tears. I quickly got up, went into the house, through the front door, in my car, and straight to the cemetery. I grabbed a blanket out of my trunk and laid in the grass under the warm sun next to Kevin's headstone.

Lesson: **Feel your feelings. Allow yourself the space to be sad. Don't judge your despair. Instead, show yourself compassion and understanding. Let grief move through you with patience and love. The only way to get out of the pain is through the pain.**

While driving home on a Saturday afternoon from a shopping trip with my girlfriend, we passed by a car with a man and a young son. They were both wearing baseball hats. It brought me back to the days when Kevin and the boys would travel to practices and games together. I became instantly sad. I missed those days. I missed Kevin. I shared my pain with my friend and told her that I wasn't sure I would make it to that night's event. I told her that I needed to go home and sit with my feelings of grief. I felt much better after a few hours and made it to the event feeling lighter and brighter.

Lesson: **Accepting help is a gift we give and receive.**

The outpouring of people that attended and donated to the Turkey Trot fundraiser for our family was a beautiful reminder that people welcome a way to embrace and support those going through difficult times. Although it may feel uncomfortable to accept, it's important to remember that giving and receiving are an exchange of love and kindness. Both sides win.

Lesson: **While we cannot control that life involves pain, we always have the power to choose how long we endure it and what we do with it.**

I made a conscious decision that sadness was not going to rent out space in my heart forever. I wanted to move the energy in a positive way. Sharing the kindness cards at the funeral services and starting the kindness matters scholarship inspired by Kevin, gave me that outlet.

Lesson: **We create stories about our experiences and convince ourselves that our perspective is the ultimate truth. Courage is when we question our reality and look deeper to uncover what we aren't willing to see.**

Asking Kevin the question, "are we searching for answers or running from the truth," was the moment that I realized reality was chasing us, and we didn't want to be caught. The result was anxiety, denial, and exhaustion.

Lesson: **Create a to-do list of who you will <u>BE</u> rather than what you will <u>DO</u>.**

I spent the first two years of Kevin's illness trying to "do," which was really my attempt to control. Finding doctors who also thought it was Lyme disease, finding therapies, treatments, and diets to get Kevin better...do, do, do. It brought me in one big circle back to the truth of having zero control. I was much more at peace when I stopped doing (attempting to control) this tragedy and began to focus on who I would "be" while going through the tragedy.

Lesson: **It may be a different happy, but happiness comes in many different forms and gets to be a strong presence in both parts – before this and after this if you choose for it to.**

My children and I have a very close, wonderful relationship. I have amazing friends and family that surround and support us every day. I am incredibly fulfilled with the many facets of my business. I have beautiful memories of a happy marriage with an amazing man who was a wonderful dad to our four children.

Lesson: 🖤 **The importance of small acts of kindness and the ability they have to change someone's day.**

What a wonderful way to start my morning ~ Eleven months after Kevin's death, I went to get my black eye (hot chocolate and espresso) at a local coffee shop as I do every morning. I was told that it was paid for by the person in front of me, and I was given a kindness card from Kevin's funeral. It was the first time the card made its way back to me. I was filled with many emotions but mostly happiness. Happiness that kindness in Kevin's name was still finding its way into the hearts of those who receive a card. I was so grateful to the unknown person that placed that kindness in mine.

Lesson: 🖤 **Situations that appear uncomfortable are growth opportunities in disguise. Grab them every chance you get! You won't recognize who you are able to become.**

Pushing myself to do things that feel scary has given me an encouraging belief in myself and has allowed me to change the narrative in my head from "I can't" and "I need help" to "Yes, I can!"

Lesson: 🖤 **The power and strength of love**

Our youngest son had Senior Night for Rec football when he was in eighth grade. This is a night to celebrate the players' final year in this program. Each family walks their player down the field while the announcer shares memories of the player. Kevin was very sick at this point, frail, and unable to walk on his own. The very field that he needed assistance walking down was the field where he had run for catches, thrown passes, instructed plays, and taught so many kids the game of football. These kids knew him as a healthy, strong athlete and coach. He didn't want to struggle down the field. You can imagine how hard that must have been. It wasn't a question for Kevin. He was going to be there for his son. Two of the older boys held each side of Kevin as he, along with our whole family, bravely walked down the field.

Lesson: 💜 **The Universe, God, Source, Angels, whatever it is for you…always has our back**

As I aimlessly pushed my cart up and down the aisles at Target, I suddenly decided that the boys needed a really good razor for Christmas. The thought sort of came out of nowhere, but a definite "need" under that year's Christmas tree. I called my best friend's husband to get some suggestions. He was so helpful and gave me a complete education on razors, shaving, and moisturizing. It was somewhere about a quarter way through our conversation that I found myself fighting back the tears. Just as abruptly as I decided the boys needed a good razor came a lump in my throat and welling in my eyes. I didn't know anything about men's razors, and I didn't want to know anything about men's razors – but I needed to know. The reality was, like it or not ~ I just needed to know ☹

Sometimes, even when we think we're over the hump and navigating through a "new normal" with a fair amount of ease, we get sucker-punched in the men's care aisle at Target. An abrupt reminder that reaching a finish line is just not how grief works.

What I found to be the most amazing and profound part of the story is what happened next. I finished our conversation, put the recommended razor in my cart, wiped my tears, and headed down the aisle toward the checkout. As I turned the corner, I looked ahead, and there, right in front of me, stood a dear friend. A friend that I happen to find a lot of comfort in. She was just there. Right there. She never disappoints and at that moment, gave me exactly what I needed – an understanding ear, a laugh, and a hug. The perfect mixture of empathy and cheer to help fill this newly exposed, broken little piece of my heart. Ahhhh...what a beautiful reminder that although sometimes raw emotion can sneak up in the most unexpected places, love will always be waiting in the next aisle.

Lesson: 🖤 **Our loved ones are always with us and communicate with us in all different ways. Let that give you peace.**

I headed to the beach one afternoon to meet my friends who recently bought a house in Cape May Court House. I was listening to Dan Harris', The 10% Happier Podcast. The episode was about the science of loss and recovery with Mary-Frances O'Connor, an expert in bereavement research. This episode had my full attention as I was cruising down the parkway. All of a sudden, as I'm completely identifying with everything they are talking about and reliving my own experience of losing Kevin, I look ahead and notice the license plate ahead of me — KJD, Kevin John Duffy. My late husband's initials. As the traffic got heavy and we came to a stop, I was able to get a photo.

What are some of the lessons hidden in your painful experiences?

_____

_____

_____

_____

_____

_____

_____

_____

_____

_____

_____

_____

_____

_____

_____

_____

_____

_____

_____

_____

_____

_____

How can you transform grief into growth?

_____

_____

_____

_____

_____

_____

_____

_____

_____

_____

_____

_____

_____

_____

_____

_____

_____

_____

_____

_____

_____

Do you believe it's possible to turn your pain into purpose? If so, how?

_____

_____

_____

_____

_____

_____

_____

_____

_____

_____

_____

_____

_____

_____

_____

_____

_____

_____

_____

_____

_____

_____

_____

"And the day came when the risk to remain tight in a bud was more painful than the risk it took to blossom."

~ Anais Nin

BLOGS

Throughout my grief journey, I have found writing to be a source of comfort. A simple and very cathartic tool for coping with periods of anxiety, stress, and sadness. Fully expressing my thoughts and feelings gave me the ability to release and understand them. It was a way of allowing my stream of consciousness to spill out and onto paper. While, at times, my feelings felt overwhelming, writing gave me an outlet and the ability to understand myself. A way of creating an inner calm during a time of outer chaos and uncertainty after Kevin's passing. I've shared some of my favorites with you.

I never thought that I would laugh again...

I never thought that I would laugh again after losing my husband.

Hope felt hopeless and so did happiness...

Certainly, grief and time played a crucial role, and SO did intention.

It's the stories we tell ourselves on autopilot, in the background of our thoughts that navigate the way we see things and the results we receive.

I hear those stories playing out in conversations about grief.

"The more I suffer, the more I prove my love."

"I'm a bad person if I move on."

Really?

That's not how I see it.

I set the intention that the more I live my best life, the more I honor my husband and teach my children that there is life after death.

Every morning before my meditation, I make intention statements and fill my heart with gratitude and I create my expectations.

"I receive joy, love and inspiration."

"I receive success and abundance."

And then I feeeeel it. My heart feels whole as I know I have created from love and decisiveness rather than fear and circumstance.

I set the intention to be the energy that I want to create.

Everything is created from intention.

Intention is energy.

It's not going to show up in the outside world until you feel it on the inside.

Choose your intentions consciously. Raise your vibration to match the outcome you desire, then focus on inspired actions that align you with that outcome.

If you want different results, raise your expectations. Change your focus.

Create new patterns. Change the stories.

There is peace and joy on the other side. We all deserve to be happy and live a fulfilled life. It's time to allow yourself that. Remind yourself that you too deserve it all. ♥

The Other First

When I think about "firsts," I feel a warm, happy feeling. What comes to mind immediately are first steps, first birthday, first day of school, first kiss, first love...the list goes on and on. All of these "firsts" are big reasons to celebrate. Firsts are always exciting, right? Of course! They are firsts!

What I never thought about was the other kind of "first." This first is the exact opposite of everything I ever thought about firsts. This first doesn't bring joy or happiness. It's nothing to celebrate but something that brings immense sadness. It's not something we anticipate with excitement; instead, it strikes us unexpectedly and sends a powerful vibration through our hearts.

I'm speaking about the "firsts" that follow losing a spouse. I wasn't prepared for some of these firsts. When you have your first child, you can purchase a book, "What to expect in the first year," or "First Time Parent." Parents who have more than one child share with you important knowledge that they have learned along the way. No one does this with "firsts" involving losing a spouse. I haven't come across a book, "What to expect the first year after losing a spouse." No one warned me about some of the things that would come up that I just never thought about or prepared for.

The things that come to mind are, of course, the obvious ~ birthday, wedding anniversary, holidays, etc. I feel like we brace ourselves for those. Where it became really difficult were not the expected events, it was the ones I never saw coming. These came out of nowhere and took my breath away.

I remember the initial "first" like it was yesterday. I was filling out paperwork at the gynecologist and came to the line *check the box*.... married, divorced, widow, single. I had to check the widow box. I hated checking the widow box!! It was an awful moment. I was by myself and I felt so sad and so broken. I would have much rather written a small essay than have checked the cold, lonely widow box. It would have read something like this...*my beautiful husband of 23 years has been called upon by God. He is deeply rooted in my soul and although not physically with me, he will forever be a part of every breath I take; he will live in my heart always.*

Ahhh...that would have felt so much better than the emptiness of checking the widow box.

The next "first" that took me by surprise was when I signed a birthday card for my dad from our family. I always signed cards, So Much Love, Kevin, Laurice, Kelly, Ty, Quinn, and Aidan xo. I quickly felt a pit in my stomach as the pen hit the paper and I suddenly realized that I would not be adding Kevin's name to this card or any other card I write again. I think my heart skipped a beat at that moment. It was something I just never thought about. It hit hard.

The last "first" that stands out and I was less than prepared for is attending an event alone and having the DJ announce, "let's slow it down. Grab your partner and join us on the dance floor." I remember sitting at my table like a deer in headlights. I didn't have a partner. He died. I forgot about slow dances. Am I going to be left at this table by myself? Of course, it turned out fine as I think everyone at my table remained seated in an attempt to cradle me without moving a muscle or saying a word. People can be so amazing!

So, although I believe "firsts" should still be thought of as beautiful moments, it's important to remember the "other first." It's necessary to be a little prepared for these moments as they are a reality of losing someone that you thought you would grow old with. Take a deep breath and know that during these times, it is important to tap into your internal reserve of hope and strength. You will find your way through. You will find your way to gracefully overcome the "other first."

Loss and Found

So often, we talk about the loss when someone we love passes away and leaves us. Of course, we do. After all, experiencing any kind of loss can be heart-wrenching and life-changing. It can rock us to our core. But is there another side to this? A piece that we're possibly missing.

At the age of 49, the time in my life that I always simply expected to be living the wonderful life my husband and I created for our family, I found myself joining a club that I never wanted to be part of - the widow's club. When you are chosen to be part of this club, the membership fee feels like the taking of your soul. There are no perks or pluses, benefits or bonuses, just pain. No one joins willingly.

In 2018, my beautiful husband of 23 years lost his battle with ALS. We celebrated his 53rd birthday, and three days later, he was called to heaven. He left behind our four amazing boys that he adored. He was their provider, protector, and playmate. He taught them manners, commitment, and honesty. He was the truest example of kindness. His standards were high, and his love knew no limits. So much loss in that last breath.

Loss comes in so many forms. Losing a partner, family member, or friend. A divorce after years of marriage. The end of a career. Perhaps the loss of yourself. No matter the form, loss equals pain.

So that's it? Enduring pain? To my surprise, actually no. What I have discovered to be true for me, is with loss, there is much that can be found. You may gasp at such a thought - the idea that there could possibly be something gained from loss. It may initially feel uncomfortable to adopt such a concept. I get it, but I ask you to challenge that thought. Take a moment and think about your loss as a whole. Not just the part about your precious loved one that has been taken from your life, or the end of your twenty-year marriage. Think about the unabbreviated experience. The entire journey. What have you found along the way? Really think about it.

I'll share some of the treasures I have collected as I courageously embrace it all:

Joy in even the smallest things as I now fully comprehend how fragile life is, and I refuse to take any of it for granted.

A reserve of strength I could tap into - I had no idea!

Kindness and love in so many people - so many amazing people in this world and right here in my own community...so blessed.

The will to move through fear and come out the other side - I am so grateful to know this about myself.

The ability to handle devastation with a certain amount of grace and even a sense of humor when appropriate. Who knew?

The power to see myself not as a victim, but as a warrior.

Listen, I'm in no way declaring that in any way this is an even exchange or a close comparison for losing a loved one, ending a marriage, or the termination of a career. But, after the dust has settled and time has passed, if you look real hard and shift your perspective just a little bit, you too may find that along with the loss, some things are actually found.

Three Graduation Caps 🎓🎓🎓

Eighteen years of everything times three...three early morning feedings, three potty training, three kids learning to read, three to watch playing sports, three to teach how to drive, and now, three graduating high school seniors.

As I prepare for a month filled with award ceremonies, prom and graduation, I feel particularly melancholy. I often find myself drifting off and reminiscing about our 18-year journey. What a ride it has been.

To my three beautiful sons ~

You arrived in this world as a team and have stuck together side by side since the day you were conceived, just as teammates would. You have shared a womb, a crib, toys, bedrooms, teams, cars, jobs, and your parents' attention. And you have done it with patience and fairness.

You have shared struggles, loss, and heartache that will be tattooed on your heart forever ~ scars that act as battle wounds to remind you of what you have been through and what you are capable of overcoming. And you have done it with strength and grace.

You have shared friendships, celebrations, and memories. You always knew how to have a good time and make things fun...sometimes too much☺ You remembered the importance of not taking yourself too seriously and having a good sense of humor. And you have done it with joy and delight.

All of these things you have done, you have done together as a team. Being together is all you have known. In a few short months, you will leave our home and head down a path of your very own. And I hope you do it with courage and excitement.

Even though you will be taking this journey at the same time, this will be an adventure that will be yours and only yours ~ something you need not share. Your own school, friends, experiences, challenges, good times, and most of all, your independence. And I am certain you will do it with care and good judgment.

A few final reminders before these last few months fly by as quickly as the past 18 years have:

Save money - remember, the best things in life are often free.

Be brave enough to say I'm sorry, I love you, and I forgive you.

Be present...live in the moment.

Give back - small offerings of service create a ripple effect.

Live with gratitude.

Be true to yourself.

Make sure your handshake is firm.

Listen to understand, not to defend.

Be kind, be kind, be kind.

And most of all, remember that individually you have each brought something so beautiful into our family. Your own magic that makes me smile. I can't wait for you to share this gift with the world. I love you.

A Big Win

So, there I was sitting on the metal bleachers with my new handmade, super comfy, wool, seat cushion. The stadium lights were radiantly shining on the new turf. The green fibers of the field were glowing bright and the stark white yard lines were as crisp as the evening air.

I was basking in excitement for this night.

For this final season.

My son was the quarterback and had a fierce throwing game.

The seasons' predictions were high and so was the energy in the stands.

In the first, second, and third plays, we were moving up the field like a beautifully choreographed dance routine.

During the fourth play, my son went down and ran off the field, holding his shoulder.

His arm popped out of the socket.

He was out for the rest of the game.

A highly recommended physical therapist worked with my son, strengthened his shoulder, and taped him up in order to get him back in the game.

It was senior night.

Also, the night we buried his nana, my mom.

He was back. He was ready. He had angels.

This was going to be his night to shine.

And then POW!

He got tackled just the right way and his OTHER shoulder popped out.

He was out for the rest of the game and permanently as the quarterback.

I was in the stands, still on my comfy wool cushion, feeling everything but comfortable.

I sat in the bleachers with my head down in disbelief. How much can this kid take?

He wanted to have his final season on a field that he loved so much, and in a game that he connected with his dad, so often

I left the game.

I was feeling so sorry for him and, if I was really being honest, sorry for me too.

As I approached the stadium exit, I realized I was in a victim mindset, feeling powerless.

I quickly shifted gears and asked the universe, "please support my desire to see this in a different way?"

"Please help me find the lesson. The opportunity. How is this happening for us and not to us? Please help me see it differently."

I arrived home and laid on my couch, anxiously waiting for my son to get home.

I was sure he was going to be frustrated, angry and unable to make sense of so much loss - his dad, nana and now an injury in his final year of the sport he loves.

He came home and sat beside me with a better than expected perspective.

His exact words, "mom, I think I would really be struggling if you weren't my mom. I listen to your stuff and I apply it to my life. It helps me a lot!"

My immediate thought: *I didn't expect you to answer so quickly, Universe. Thank you!*

My son didn't have a successful season on the football field, but he was living an internal win that would last a lifetime.

Sometimes our definition of amazing is different from the universe's.

It's this or something better.

Thank you for something better...

Hope

While going through the core of Kevin's illness and enduring some very difficult days, I would often walk up to the park and sit on the rocks overlooking the lake and meditate. During that time, the lake had been dredged. It was an unpleasant empty hole of dirt. I was disappointed but chose to look beyond it. Since Kevin's passing, I haven't been able to get back to the rocks. Yesterday I found some time and made my way back. The lake was filled and looked more beautiful than I ever remembered. The water gave off a silver-blue hue in the bright light of the morning sun peeking its way behind the gracefully shaped clouds. Its soft ripple almost felt hypnotic. I sat on the rocks, but instead of meditating, I just took in the amazing view. I reflected back on how the empty hole that was in front of me during those tough times was also inside of me. Revisiting the lake and witnessing all its renewed magnificence filled my heart with hope. I felt it signified that after devastation, life can be beautiful again. That the empty hole we feel during various challenges does get refilled with calmness, beauty, and peace.

A letter to you, my beautiful reader!

So here we are almost five years later...

I have, with great effort, caught my breath and committed myself to breathing life into loss with so many beautiful women who are still finding their way through this difficult journey. Loss comes in so many forms. There is the loss of a partner, the loss of a marriage, the loss of feeling like mom when your last child leaves home, and the list goes on and on...

No loss can be compared to another. For the person experiencing it, loss has taken their breath away. The painful question of why and the uncertainty of what's next may feel not only debilitating but also terrifying. Rebuilding can feel daunting and unbearable. For others it can feel frustrating. Either way, it has the ability to keep you stuck.

Sometimes grief comes not from losing someone else but from losing yourself. You might be constantly searching for a compass to point you to your purpose. Wanting to step out of the darkness and into the light of your authentic self. So tired of living life by the playbook that has been passed down to you. Drowning in the *should's*. Fed up with meeting everyone else's needs without ever considering your own.

I get you. I've got you. In many ways, I was you. And as I reflect on the death of my beautiful husband, I am here to remind you that you have all the answers. You have all the strength. You have all the power within you. You have the ability to spread your wings and fly high no matter what the circumstance of your loss.

Although I cannot take away the pain, I can resuscitate your hope. I can be an example of what's possible. I can grab your hand and walk this journey with you or cheer you on from the sideline. Either way, know this - I'm in your corner, I'm rooting for you, and I love you, for you are me, and I am you...we are one.